MODERN INDIA

ITS PROBLEMS AND THEIR SOLUTION

MODERN INDIA

ITS PROBLEMS AND THEIR SOLUTION

V. H. RUTHERFORD

GYAN

Published by

GYAN

Gyan Publishing House
5, Ansari Road
Daryaganj, New Delhi-110002
Phone: 011-47034999, 9811692060
E-mail: books@gyanbooks.com

Distribution Network
gyanbooks.com
India, USA, Canada, UK, Australia

ISBN: 978-93-7097-646-7 (PB)

First Published, 1927

2nd Impression 2025

Printed at: Gyan Press, Delhi.

MODERN INDIA ITS PROBLEMS AND THEIR SOLUTION

Author: V. H. RUTHERFORD

MODERN
INDIA

Modern India

Its problems and their solution

By

V. H. Rutherford

M.A., MB., Cantab.

India. Do you know why English soldiers are called goddams?

Gandhi. No. Every one calls them goddams.

India. It is because they are always calling on their God to condemn their souls to perdition. That is what goddam means in their language. How do you like it?

Gandhi. God will be merciful to them, and they will act like good children, *when they go back to the country He made for them, and made them for*. I have heard the tales of Clive and Hastings. The moment they touched the soil of our country the devil entered into them and made them black fiends; but at home, in the place made for them by God, they were good. It is always so. If I went into England to conquer England and tried to live there and speak her language, the devil would enter into me; and when I was old I should shudder to remember the wickednesses I did.

With apologies to G. Bernard Shaw.

CONTENTS

INTRODUCTION

My object in writing this book is to right Great Britain in the eyes of India and of the world by prevailing upon my countrymen to grant complete self-government to India.

By denying self-government to one-fifth of the human race we lay ourselves open to the charge of being the greatest barrier to freedom and progress in the world.

The Montagu-Chelmsford Reforms, instead of conferring responsible government upon India, strengthened and consolidated the powers of the British bureaucracy behind sham parliaments. Indian Nationalists regard these reforms as a Himalayan hoax and a breach of honour, and in consequence many of them decline to co-operate in working them.

In embodying the evil principle of "communal electorates" in the reforms, the British Parliament made itself responsible to a large extent for the outbursts of communal strife between Hindus and Moslems. Immediately after the Armistice India's stupendous services in the Great War were repaid by the inauguration of a reign of terror in India and the awful massacre of Amritsar, perpetrated by a British general and condoned by the British rulers in India and by the House of Lords in England, with the result that British rule in India is hated more than ever.

Our neglect of education for the masses, of sanitation and medical services in the villages, of housing in the towns, and our comparative neglect of agricultural and industrial development, stamp our rule as both "inefficient" and "injurious."

Our forefathers took India by the "mailed fist" for the purpose of exploiting her resources, and we hold India in subjection to-day for the same immoral purpose.

Our imposition by force of European standards upon Indian civilisation has been fraught with disaster to moral progress and to a higher standard of civilisation.

Our Indian Empire has poisoned us with the virus of Imperialism, has lowered our standard of moral values at home and abroad, and fostered in us the spirit of arrogance, intolerance, greed and dishonesty, degrading our national life.

One evil leads to another. In order to tighten our hold on India we have rattled into barbarism by seizing Egypt, Cyprus, Aden, Somaliland, Mesopotamia, etc.; by partitioning Persia, which evil has been undone since the war; by consolidating our South African Empire by wars; by making a naval base at Singapore; by waging wars against Afghanistan; and by indulging in armaments on such a scale that we vie with France as the greatest military and naval Power in the world.

Our emasculation of 300 millions of people by preventing their natural evolution and by depriving them of control of the administration, military and political services, of their own country, stands condemned as an unpardonable offence.

God made the nations, and man made the empires in frustration of His designs, and in consequence the wrath of God has been visited on every empire from time immemorial. Who so bold as to deny that the Great War was the Nemesis of European empires, competing for "spots in the sun," empires which had defied, and continue to defy, God by enslaving other nations with or without the camouflage of "mandate"?

Fortunately for freedom, the British Empire has not escaped "the mills of God," which ground off America first, then Canada and South Africa, and most recently Ireland, which, with Australia and New Zealand, are free and independent nations to-day in the British Commonwealth.

We must distinguish between "empire" and "commonwealth." Empire is an artificial amalgamation of nations held together by the "sword" against the will of the People, while Commonwealth is a natural union of peoples, cemented together by common consent, by common ties and ideals, in which union each group of peoples enjoys absolute freedom to work out its own salvation.

Like the late President Wilson, I should like to distinguish between Peoples and Governments, because the British people, though responsible for and punished for the acts of their Government, are largely ignorant of the crimes of the Government in India, and are never consulted on the policy pursued in India, and even their representatives in Parliament are rarely consulted; and, further, the people are deceived by the hypocritical pretences of Government that we rule India for the good of Indians and not for our own national benefit; that we hold India in bondage as trustees, forgetting to add that Indians denounce us as "*self-appointed*" and "*fraudulent*" trustees.

As far as the outside world is concerned, history reveals the character of our pretended trusteeship in the fact that India has been used as a pawn by Great Britain in her imperial designs upon China, Afghanistan, Persia, Mesopotamia and Egypt, making Indians hated by Asiatics and Africans, and robbing Indians of self-respect by incriminating them and their country, by using the Indian army in these attacks upon the liberty and independence of other countries.

How " fraudulent " has been our " self-appointed " trusteeship in India was exposed when Warren Hastings was tried for seven years before the House of Lords on charges of " high crimes and misdemeanours," when, in spite of the overwhelming evidence of gross misrule, that assembly dishonoured itself and England by whitewashing him. Recently the House of Lords published to the world the fraudulency of our trusteeship by repeating its earlier error in extolling the " high crimes and misdemeanours " of O'Dwyer and Dyer.

Queen Victoria, when she assumed in 1858 " the government hitherto administered in trust for us by the ' Honourable East India Company,' " issued a proclamation reiterating the assurance given by Parliament in 1833 that " as far as may be " her Indian subjects, " of whatever creed or race," would be freely and impartially admitted to offices in the service of the Crown. From 1833 to 1926 is nearly one hundred years, and Indians are still waiting for the fulfilment of these royal and parliamentary pledges.

Lord Lytton, who was Viceroy of India in the halcyon days of Disraeli, who waged aggressive wars against the Afghans to bring Afghanistan within the orbit of imperial Britain, let the cat out of the bag in a peculiarly frank and cynical manner.

Referring to the claims and expectations of Indians

based upon the solemn declarations of both Queen Victoria and Parliament, Lord Lytton wrote :—

> " We all know that these claims and expectations never can or will be fulfilled. We have to choose between prohibiting them and cheating them, and we have chosen the least straightforward course. . . . Since I am writing confidentially, I do not hesitate to say that both the Government of England and of India appear to me up to the present moment unable to answer satisfactorily the charge of having taken every means in their power of breaking to the heart the words of promise they had uttered to the ear."

I now deliberately accuse the British Government, which passed the so-called reforms of 1919, " of having taken every means in their power of breaking to the heart the words of promise they had uttered to the ear," promises of " responsible government," of " partnership," and of all the lovely things that would accrue to India as an ally in the Great War for Freedom.

Sir Austen Chamberlain tells us that we are not a " logical " people, but the more important question now arises whether we are " honest." Parliament, by the 1919 Government of India Act, made it clear without a possible shadow of doubt that our politicians and would-be statesmen were " dishonest." The mere fact that Lord Birkenhead, the arch-conspirator of rebellion in Ulster, is Secretary of State for India, where " patriotism " is a crime punishable at law, proves His Majesty's Government to be " dishonest " as well as " illogical," unless Mr. Baldwin appointed him with the definite intention to lead Indians out of bondage to the promised land of self-government.

I love my country, and my love for her impels me to appeal to the higher and nobler elements in her nature, to clear herself of "dishonesty" and "hypocrisy."

The problem of governing ourselves is big enough without undertaking the government of India.

The history of our own country reveals the incapacity of our ruling classes to govern justly. The present condition of the masses in general, and of the miners in particular, is a homely illustration of the failure of British statesmanship, and of the vanity of Imperialism.

Our Empire has not saved us from a low and degrading standard of life, but has depressed it more, and aggravated the extremes between the poor and the rich.

Instead of England being a land fit for heroes to live in, it is a pleasure ground and an exploiting ground for the rich, too many of whom have amassed their wealth at the expense of the poor of India and the poor of England.

Incapable of governing ourselves well, how can we govern others?

What right have we to govern others *without their consent?* Therein constitutes the gravity of our crime. "Like little wanton boys that swim on bladders, we have ventured in a sea of vain pomp and glory, but far beyond our depth."

Clothed in self-righteousness, our besetting sin, we strut like Pharisees over the imperial stage, and thank God that we are not like other Imperialists—Greeks, Romans, and Huns (ancient and modern). A little sober thinking might suggest to us that we are greater sinners against a world of peace and goodwill than our imperial brothers the Greeks, Romans, and Huns, for they had not the advantage of the light and lessons to mankind which flow from Calvary, the French and the Russian Revolutions.

Living in glass houses, we denounce German and Austrian Imperialists for doing in Alsace-Lorraine and Italy what we do on a bigger scale in India, Egypt and elsewhere.

The rod of empire wielded by Britons injures and pains economically, physically, and morally Indians, Egyptians and others in the same way that the rod of empire wielded by Germans and Austrians injured and pained Alsatians, Lorrainers and Italians. To evade the rod of empire in the hands of Germans over our own bodies and souls what sacrifices did we make! To get rid of the rod of empire was ostensibly the great aim of the Great War, and is the greatest need of the world to-day. Since that war ended the rod of empire has flourished fiercely in India.

That which we abhor ourselves should we not abhor equally when applied to others?

Ought we not as a nation to walk humbly before God, to confess our sins with contrition, and to turn our hearts and minds from the lure of empire, with all its falseness, baseness and brutality, to the beauty of holiness, of human brotherhood and human freedom? Would it not be better for England, for her moral and spiritual grandeur, for her influence in the world, to be a doorkeeper in the house of God than to dwell in the tents of imperial wickedness?

India is rightfully struggling to be free, and England is wrongfully resisting this legitimate and praiseworthy aim. How much longer is England going to kick against the pricks?

The great renunciation must come one day, the renunciation of the empire of the sword and of the empire of selfishness, which some would translate as the empire of capitalism. Until that day comes poor demented humanity must continue to wade through seas of blood and extortion and torture.

The greatest service that Great Britain can render the world now is to set her own house in order by ceasing to play the part of gaoler and exploiter to one-fifth of the human race.

Let England act on the admonition of her greatest son, and—

> " Fling away ambition :
> By that sin fell the angels ; how can man then,
> The image of his Maker, hope to win by't ?
> Love thyself last : cherish those hearts that hate thee ;
> Corruption wins not more than honesty.
> Still in thy right hand carry gentle peace,
> Be just, and fear not :
> Let all the ends thou aim'st at be thy country's,
> Thy God's, and truth's."

MODERN INDIA

CHAPTER I

MAHATMA GANDHI

The Non-Co-operation Movement

THE history of Indians overseas may be read in the life of Mahatma Gandhi from 1893 to 1914, when he fought and won the first round in the battle of freedom for Indians in South Africa, and in consequence for Indians in the British Empire, where they were treated as helots, and the history of India from 1919 to the present day in his struggle for her freedom.

What Mazzini was to Italy, what Parnell and Davitt were to Ireland, what Washington was to America, and what the Carpenter of Nazareth was to the poor of Palestine, Mahatma Gandhi is to India.

With brilliancy and power, with simplicity and fidelity, Romain Rolland has written the life of this great spiritual, social and political Messiah, "qui a soulevé trois cent millions d'hommes, ébranlé le British Empire, et inauguré dans la politique humaine le plus puissant mouvement depuis pres de deux mille ans." [1]

A little man, frail as an aspen leaf, with large protruding ears, short moustache, closely cropped hair,

[1] "Who has uplifted three hundred million men, shaken the British Empire, and inaugurated in human policy the most powerful movement since well-nigh two thousand years."

luminous dark eyes, and a smile made sweet of all accord, I felt in the presence of one whom love of God had blessed, and one who loved his fellow-man. A white loin-cloth falling short of his knees, and a wrap made of cotton homespun hanging over his shoulders, laid bare part of his chest and the whole of his attenuated legs and feet, shod in wooden sandals.

Eating mostly rice and fruits, and drinking only water and milk, Gandhi frequently fasts, especially when any of his followers sin against the light.

Reminding him of the preciousness of his life to India, I gently admonished him, as a medical man, on the danger of long fasting, when he reproved me with a sweet smile, as much as to say, "You doctors don't know everything, and as for me, I must be about my Master's business." I had noticed two or three days before that when he addressed upwards of 10,000 people at the Indian National Congress he sat in a chair because of the feebleness of his body. Without any apparent effort, without any of the demonstration common to impassioned orators, without ringing the changes of intonation, speaking with deep conviction, calmly and slowly, in simple lucid language, he appealed chiefly to the intelligence of his vast audience, which he held riveted in rapt attention.

Mocking British officials, who used to taunt the Nationalists and Swarajists as a party confined to the intelligentsia, now admit that Mahatma Gandhi has awakened the national spirit and the national consciousness among the masses and united them as they have never been before in their legitimate demand for self-government.

Admired by all, save one or two who for a piece of silver have not hesitated to betray him, beloved and worshipped by the common people as saint and saviour in spite of his request not to be regarded as supernatural, the Mahatma is the "uncrowned King of India."

Mahatma is the title bestowed on Gandhi by the people of India, which means "great soul"—from *maha*, great, and *aima*, soul—and can be traced back to the Upanishads, where it designates the Supreme Being and, by communion with knowledge and love, those who unite themselves to Him.

Educated at the Universities of Ahmedabad and London, he was called to the Bar in England. After practising as a barrister for a year in Bombay, he went to Pretoria to plead an important case in 1893.

In Natal he suffered gross insults from white men possessed by the devil, by Xenophobia, by race hatred, who had neither the wit nor the will to see deeper than the colour of his skin; he was thrown out of hotels and trains, and struck and kicked. In consequence of this treatment he would have returned at once to India had he not entered into engagements for a year.

At the end of that time, in obedience to the dictates of his conscience and the heart-beats of love, he renounced a lucrative practice of £5,000 to £6,000 a year, embraced poverty like Francis of Assisi, initiated an agricultural colony on Tolstoian lines near Durban, and there lived in common with his poor and persecuted fellow-countrymen, undertaking servile tasks, in order that he might lead them out of the economic and political bondage and iniquitous cruelty of the white man and the white man's government.

As related in another chapter, Indians in South Africa were not only subjected to "overwhelming taxation, humiliating police restrictions, public outrages, and sometimes lynching, pillage, and destruction," but to anti-Indian legislation, against which Gandhi organised the Indian Congress of Natal, an association for the education of Indians; a journal, *Indian Opinion*, published in English and in three Indian languages; public demonstrations of protest; monster petitions to the Imperial Parliament; and the Non-Resistance or Passive Resistance Movement, which Rolland described as " a religious strike, against which all violence breaks itself, as that of imperial Rome against the early Christians."

The Mahatma beat the record of Christians by not only pardoning but loving his enemies, for he formed an Indian Red Cross service during the Boer War, which was twice mentioned for its bravery under fire, and he organised a hospital in 1904, when the plague broke out at Johannesburg, and he ran an ambulance during the war against the natives in 1906, when the Natal Government thanked him publicly. The same Government, a little later, put him in prison, condemning him to solitary confinement and hard labour.

Gandhi experienced every kind of suffering, being incarcerated four times, beaten by the mob, and once left for dead.

In 1909 General Smuts declared that he would never erase from the statute book a measure injurious to Indians; but by 1914 Gandhi's gospel of love and conscientious objection by passive resistance conquered the General, who avowed that he was happy to remove it, thereby abolishing the capitation tax of £3 per house and permitting Indians to reside in Natal as free men.

After twenty years of ceaseless struggle and sacrifice Mahatma Gandhi not only won a celebrated victory for Indians in South Africa and in the British Empire, but a far greater and more valuable world victory for his cherished principles of "Love" and "Non-Violence," which he put in the following phraseology: "Our object is friendship with the whole world. Non-violence has come to men, and it will remain. It is the enunciation of peace on earth."

This epic struggle and epic victory won by one man against innumerable odds has been too little sung in England, which once worshipped heroes in the great moral and progressive fights, but now prefers Empire-builders who break every law, human and divine.

His mission accomplished in South Africa, and his spurs won as a leader of men, Mahatma Gandhi returned to India in 1914 to support and strengthen the hands of those noble and devoted patriots Gokhali and Lokamanya Bal Gangadhar Tilak in the fight for India's freedom. At this date, or even before, the spiritual leadership passed to the Mahatma, while C. R. Das and Motilal Nehru right loyally fulfilled the functions of political leaders of the National Congress.

At this point it would be interesting to note that if the British Government in England and the British rulers in India had been loyal to their pledges and avoided the policy of the "mailed fist" in India, the Mahatma, who was a religious devotee first and a politician second, would probably never have been driven into what the bureaucrats are pleased to call the Extremist Camp (that is, the camp which makes the greatest sacrifices for the liberty of their country), and would never have inaugurated the Non-Co-operation Campaign, and one of the darkest and most disgraceful chapters of British rule in India would never have needed to be written.

In support of this contention British Imperialists must be reminded of the fact that when the Great War broke out Gandhi came over to England to raise an ambulance corps, believing, as he himself said, that he was a "citizen of the Empire," and that "no Englishman had co-operated more strictly than he with the Empire during twenty-nine years of public activity. Four times he had endangered his life for England. . . . Until 1919 he had advocated co-operation with sincere conviction."

When the Great War broke out, India rose as one man to help England against Germany instead of rising as one man, according to German expectations, to fight for her own freedom. The Declaration of War aims, namely, "To make the world safe for democracy," "The protection of small nationalities," and "Self-determination for all peoples," captured the minds and hearts of the people of India, who read in it their title to freedom and self-government.

In August, 1917, the Secretary of State for India (Mr. Montagu) promised "responsible government to India within the British Empire," and the following winter visited India for the purpose of learning Indian public opinion and consulting the Viceroy, Lord Chelmsford, with regard to ways and means of carrying out this solemn pledge.

On April 2nd, 1918, the Prime Minister (Mr. Lloyd George), alarmed by the danger confronting the Allied armies, sent a message to India reminding her of "the intention of the rulers of Germany to establish a tyranny not only over Europe, but over Asia as well," and asking "every lover of freedom and law" to play his part in preventing "the menace spreading to the East and gradually engulfing the world," and hoping that India " will add to the laurels it has already won," and " be the bulwark which will save Asia." Mahatma Gandhi, on behalf of Indian reformers of all shades of opinion, joined the War Conference at Delhi on April 27th, 1918, when the King-Emperor's message declared that " the need of the Empire is India's opportunity."

India contributed in money not less than £130,000,000, and in men 1,457,000, and her services were recognised and spoken of in the most eulogistic terms by the Viceroy and the Prime Minister of England. India awaited confidently the reward of her fidelity after the Armistice.

India's goodwill and stupendous sacrifices to win the war were repaid by the British bureaucracy, first, by suspension instead of extension of the existing liberties; by abuse of the Defence of India Act, under whose dangerous provisions a large number of Indians of unblemished character, along with Mrs. Besant, were arrested and interned; and, secondly, by the introduction of the Rowlatt Bills in February, 1919, in the Imperial Legislative Council at Delhi.

The object of these black Bills was to take away trial by jury, and assessors in cases of sedition, holding trials *in camera* after the Star Chamber pattern, admitting evidence without cross-examination, and unrecorded by the court, and, worst of all, reserving to the executive the right and power not only to restrict the liberty of the subject by demanding securities with or without sureties, by restricting his residence, or requiring notification of change of residence, and demanding abstention from certain acts, such as engaging in journalism, attending meetings, etc., but also to deprive him of all liberty by arresting and confining him.

The whole country protested against this unwarranted encroachment on the fundamental rights of citizens, but the cruel and callous Government of India passed the Bills into an Act in March, 1919, whereupon some members (Lord Sinha and Sir Sankaran Nair) of the Imperial Legislative Council resigned their seats, and Gandhi led a campaign of refusal to obey these laws, laying down the principle that "in this struggle we will faithfully follow the truth and refrain from violence to life, person, or property."

Satyagraha [1] is the name which Gandhi himself gave to the movement, which lasted four years and shook the British Empire as it had not been shaken since the American War of Independence.

The Satyagraha was a " constitutional opposition " in the opinion of Romain Rolland, whose disinterested and unbiassed judgment should have weight even with Imperialists, against an " unjust " and " dishonouring law," and if that did not suffice to re-establish justice, the members of the Satyagraha reserved to themselves the right to extend their disobedience to other laws, and even to withdraw entirely their co-operation from the Government.

Gandhi's philosophy taught his disciples that violence never convinces, that they must convince by the radiance of love, by abnegation, by sufferings, freely and joyously accepted, which Rolland pronounces as " irresistible propaganda " ; " by it the

Satya=righteous ; *graha*=endeavour. Some critics maintain that this derivation violates Sanskrit laws. Gandhi said its root meaning is " holding on to truth," hence truth-force.

cross of Christ and of His little flock conquered the Roman Empire."

Christian Imperialists—how a Christian can be an Imperialist has always been incomprehensible to the writer—will learn with surprise that Gandhi attributes his idea of Passive Resistance as the most righteous weapon for the attainment of justice and liberty, whether applied to individuals or nations, to reading the Sermon on the Mount, which made him overflow with joy, and which the "Bhagavad Gita," one of the sacred books of the Hindus, fortified, and "The Kingdom of God is in You," by Tolstoi, supported.

As there is considerable confusion in English minds regarding Gandhi's methods, the following translation of an important passage from Romain Rolland's book is submitted :—

> "The term 'Satyagraha' had been invented by Gandhi in South Africa in order to distinguish his action from Passive Resistance. It is necessary to insist with the greatest force upon that distinction, for it is precisely by 'passive resistance' (or by 'non-resistance') that Europeans define Gandhi's movement. Nothing is falser. No man in the world has more aversion to passivity than this tireless fighter, who is one of the most heroic types of 'unyielding' (Resistant). The spirit of his movement is Active Resistance, through energy fired by love, by faith, and by sacrifice. And this triple energy is expressed in the word *Satyagraha*."

Gandhi himself defined it as "the triumph of truth by soul-force and love. . . . Non-violence does not mean meek submission to the will of the evil-doer, but the pitting of one's whole soul against the will of the tyrant. . . . I would risk violence a thousand times rather than emasculation of the race. . . . Where there is only a choice between cowardice and violence, I advise violence. I cultivate the quiet courage of dying without killing. But to him who has not this courage I advise that of killing and being killed rather than that of shamefully fleeing from danger. For he who runs away commits mental violence; he runs away because he has not the courage to be killed while he kills."

In the perpetual war of principles the Mahatma reflects the ideal expressed by Krishna in the "Bhagavad Gita" when he exhorted his disciple Arjuna to "stand up and fight," only Gandhi limits himself and his disciples to the weapon of love. "The hardest fibre must melt in the fire of love. If it does not melt, it is because the fire is not strong enough."

On March 23rd, 1919, Mahatma Gandhi issued his manifesto fixing April 6th for the observance of an all-India *hartal* (stoppage of work), and as a day of fasting, prayer and penance. The *hartal* was observed at Delhi on March 30th, when a riot ensued from a quarrel between a demonstrator and the stall-keeper at the railway station, and the military police and a small military force shot some people. On April 6th the *hartal* was observed, quietly and without outward incident, by rich and poor, high and low, educated and uneducated, villagers and townsmen, throughout India. India had rediscovered her soul.

Whilst proceeding to Delhi to enlighten the people upon their duties and to relieve the sufferings of those who had been shot down Gandhi was served with an order not to enter the Punjab or Delhi, and on his refusal to obey the order he was arrested and sent back to Bombay. The news of his arrest exasperated public opinion throughout the country, and Sir Michael O'Dwyer, the Governor of the Punjab, added to his arbitrary and reactionary methods the folly of deporting on April 10th Drs. Kitchlew and Satyapal, Amritsar's two popular leaders, when a large body of men, who were proceeding to the house of the Deputy Commissioner in order to ask for the release of their leaders, were fired upon, and some were fatally wounded. A riot at once ensued, when two Europeans were murdered, two ladies assaulted, and some banks and Government offices burnt and looted.

The Massacre of Amritsar

General Dyer occupied Amritsar with troops on the night of April 11th, and no untoward incident happened either on the 11th or 12th.

The following description, with abbreviations, is taken from the report of the Committee of Inquiry appointed by the Government of India (four months after the events), and presided over by Lord Hunter, lately Solicitor-General for Scotland :—

" *First News of a Meeting*

" About 1 p.m. General Dyer heard that the people intended to hold a big meeting about 4.30 p.m. In reply to the question 'Why did you not take measures to prevent its being held ?' General Dyer answered : 'I went there as soon as I could. I had to think the matter out ; I had to organise my forces and make up my mind as to where I might put my pickets. I thought I had done enough to make the crowd not meet. If they were going to meet, I had to consider the military situation and make up my mind what to do, which took me a certain amount of time.' "

With regard to General Dyer's proclamation prohibiting public meetings, the report remarks: "It does not appear what steps were taken to ensure its publication."

"At the Bagh

"About four o'clock in the afternoon of April 13th General Dyer received definite information that a meeting was being held at Jallianwala Bagh, contrary to the terms of the proclamation issued by him that morning. He then proceeded through the city with a number of pickets, which he left at prearranged places, and a special force of twenty-five Gurkhas and twenty-five Baluchis armed with rifles, forty Gurkhas armed only with kukris, and two armoured cars. On arriving at Jallianwala Bagh he entered with his force by a narrow entrance which was not sufficiently wide to allow the cars to pass. They were accordingly left in the street outside.

"The Jallianwala Bagh is not in any sense a garden, as its name would suggest. It is a rectangular piece of unused ground, covered to some extent by building material and *débris*. It is almost entirely surrounded by the walls of buildings. The entrances and exits to it are few and imperfect. It seems to be frequently used to accommodate large gatherings of people. At that end of the Bagh by which General Dyer entered there is raised ground on each side of the entrance. A large crowd had gathered at the opposite end of the Bagh, and were being addressed by a man on a raised platform about 100 yards from where General Dyer stationed his troops. According to the report sent by General Dyer to the Adjutant-General after the occurrence, the crowd numbered about 6,000. It is probable that it was much more numerous, and that from 10,000 to 20,000 people were assembled.

"*Firing*

"As soon as General Dyer entered the Bagh he stationed twenty-five troops on one side of the higher ground at the entrance, and twenty-five troops on the other side. Without giving the crowd any warning to disperse, which he considered unnecessary, as they were in breach of his proclamation, he ordered his troops to fire, and the firing was continued for about ten minutes. There is no evidence as to the nature of the address to which the audience was listening. None of them were provided with firearms, although some of them may have been carrying sticks.

"*Casualties*

"As soon as firing commenced the crowd began to disperse. In all 1,650 rounds were fired by the troops. The firing was individual, and not volley firing. Many casualties occurred among the crowd. As General Dyer, when the firing ceased, immediately marched his troops back to the Ram Bagh, just outside the city, there was no means at the time of forming a correct estimate of the number killed and wounded. At first it was thought that about 200 had been killed. Recently an investigation into the number has been completed by the Government with the assistance of a list compiled by the Allahabad Social Service League. As a result of this investigation it was discovered that approximately 379 people were killed. No figure was given for the wounded, but this number may be taken as probably three times as great as the number killed.

" After the firing at Jallianwala Bagh no serious outbreak occurred in Amritsar.

" *Criticism of this Action*

" General Dyer's action in firing on the crowd is open to criticism in two respects: first, that he started firing without giving the people who had assembled a chance to disperse; and second, that he continued firing for a substantial period of time after the crowd had commenced to disperse.

" *Firing while Crowd dispersing*

" In continuing to fire for so long as he did it appears to us that General Dyer committed a grave error. General Dyer said: 'I fired, and continued to fire, until the crowd dispersed, and I consider this is the least amount of firing which would produce the necessary moral and widespread effect it was my duty to produce if I was to justify my action. If more troops had been at hand the casualties would have been greater in proportion. It was no longer a question of merely dispersing the crowd, but one of producing a sufficient moral effect from a military point of view not only on those who were present, but more especially throughout the Punjab. There could be no question of undue severity. . . . It was a horrible duty I had to perform. I think it was a merciful thing. I thought that I should shoot well and shoot strong, so that I, or anybody else, should not have to shoot again.' "

The comment of the Hunter Committee on this is, " In our view this was, unfortunately, a mistaken conception of his duty."

"*Attention to Wounded*

"On being questioned as to whether he had taken any measures for the relief of the wounded General Dyer explained that the hospitals were open and the medical officers were there. His own words were: 'Certainly not. It was not his job. Hospitals were open, and they could have gone to them.'

"*Effect*

"The action taken by General Dyer has also been described by others as having saved the situation in the Punjab, and having averted a rebellion on a scale similar to the Mutiny. It does not, however, appear to us possible to draw this conclusion, particularly in view of the fact that it is not proved that a conspiracy to overthrow British power had been formed prior to the outbreaks."

In the company of some of Amritsar's most distinguished citizens, the writer visited this enclosure—a veritable death-trap—the scene of the massacre, which surpasses that of Glencoe in cruelty, and learnt more harrowing details; for instance, how the killed included boys of thirteen and fourteen years of age.

"*Conspiracy*

"On the evidence before us there is nothing to show that the outbreak in the Punjab was part of a prearranged conspiracy to overthrow the British Government in India by force."

This is the conclusion of the Hunter Committee upon an atrocity which, if it had been committed by Abdul "the Damned," would have made Great Britain ring with denunciation from John o' Groat's to Land's End.

How unnecessary it was, how easily avoidable it was, the reader may judge from General Dyer's admission before the Committee :—

" I think it is quite possible I could have dispersed the crowd without firing, but they would have come back again and laughed, and I should have made what I consider to be a fool of myself."

Martial Law and a Reign of Terror

Subsequently to the massacre, on April 14th, martial law was declared in Amritsar, Lahore, Gujerat, and Lyallpur districts, and a reign of terror ensued, which Rolland describes : " Aviators threw bombs on disarmed crowds. The most honourable citizens were dragged before military tribunals, publicly whipped, compelled to crawl on their bellies in a public street, and subjected to shameful humiliations. One would have said that a wave of madness swept over the English tyrants. As if the law of non-violence proclaimed by India had had for its first effect to exasperate the violent from Europe even to frenzy! Gandhi did not ignore it. He had not promised to lead his people to victory by a white road. He had promised them the path of blood. And the day of the Jallianwalla Bagh was only the day of baptism."

According to the report of the Hunter Committee, 114 cases were tried in Lahore, involving 852 accused, before Martial Law Commissioners, who tried cases unfettered by the ordinary recognised rules of procedure or laws of evidence. Of these 581 were convicted ; 108 persons condemned to death, 265 transported for life, 2 sentenced to transportation for other periods, 5 to imprisonment for ten years, 85 for seven, and 104 for shorter periods. Substantial alteration of these sentences was made by the local Government. Of the 108 death sentences only 23 have been maintained. Of the remaining 85 sentences 23 have been commuted to transportation for life, 26 to rigorous imprisonment for ten years, 14 to seven years, 1 to six years, 10 to five years, and 11 to periods ranging from one to four years. Of the sentences of transportation for life 2 only were maintained; in 5 the Government ordered immediate release of the convicts, while the remaining 258 sentences were commuted to terms of imprisonment, 2 for ten years and the remainder for periods ranging from one to seven.

The Congress Punjab Inquiry

The Punjab Sub-Committee of the Indian National Congress appointed M. K. Gandhi, C. R. Das, A. S. Tyabji and M. R. Jayakar, all eminent barristers-at-law, to make an independent inquiry, and to report. Unfortunately, the Hunter Committee had been unable to examine the evidence produced by this weighty committee.

The following are amongst the most important conclusions contained in the valuable report of this committee :—

1. The people of the Punjab were incensed against Sir M. O'Dwyer's administration by reason of his studied contempt and distrust of the educated classes, and by reason of the cruel and compulsory methods adopted during the war for obtaining recruits and monetary contributions, and by his suppression of public opinion by gagging the local press.

2. The arrest and internment of Mr. Gandhi and

the arrests and deportations of Drs. Kitchlew and Satyapal were unjustifiable, and were the direct cause of hysterical popular excitement.

3. The Jallianwalla Bagh massacre was a calculated piece of inhumanity towards utterly innocent and unarmed men and children, and unparalleled for its ferocity in the history of modern British administration.

4. No reasonable cause had been shown to justify the introduction of martial law.

5. The martial law tribunals resulted in abortion of justice on a wide scale, and caused moral and material sufferings to hundreds of men and women.

6. The "crawling" order and other fancy punishments were unworthy of a civilised Administration, and were symptomatic of the moral degradation of their inventors.

7. It is our deliberate opinion that Sir M. O'Dwyer, General Dyer, Colonel Johnson, Colonel O'Brien, Mr. Bosworth Smith, Rai Ram Sud and Malik Saieb Khan have been guilty of such illegalities that they deserve to be *impeached*, but we purposely refrain from advising any such course, because we believe that India can only gain by waiving the right. Future purity will be sufficiently guaranteed by the dismissal of the officials concerned.

8. We are of the opinion that the Viceroy, Lord Chelmsford, should be recalled, because he endorsed the action of the Punjab Government without inquiry; he clothed the officials with indemnity in indecent haste; he failed to inform the public and the Imperial Government of the full nature of the Jallianwalla Bagh massacre, or the subsequent acts done under martial law, etc.

Condonation of the Massacre

Immediately after the massacre Sir Michael O'Dwyer, the Lieutenant-Governor of the Punjab, allowed a telegram to be sent to General Dyer: "Your action correct. Lieutenant-Governor approves"; and the Government of India, "anticipating the inquiry of the Hunter Committee," rushed an Indemnity Bill by their official *bloc* through the Imperial Council, in the face of the strong protests of the non-official members. The result of this is that, so far as India is concerned, officials responsible for excesses and abuse of authority are immune in the Indian courts from prosecution in civil suits for anything done under martial law in good faith.

In England Dyer was publicly presented with a sword of honour, and was hailed in the House of Lords as a saviour of empire because he had given Indian patriots a lesson in Prussianism.

The Khalifat Question

Next to the Rowlatt Act and the reign of terror arising out of it, the question of the Khalifat disturbed the people of India. Indian Mussulmans to the number of 70 millions had to choose between England and Turkey, whose sultan was the defender of their faith. They backed England on the Prime Minister's assurance of immunity of the holy places in Arabia and Mesopotamia, regarding which Mr. Lloyd George said: "Nor are we fighting to deprive Turkey of its capital or of the rich and renowned lands of Asia Minor and Thrace, which are predominantly Turkish in race."

Khalifat conferences were held at Delhi, Amritsar and Bombay in 1919 and 1920, and a manifesto warned the Governments of India and England against violating "the deepest religious feelings of Mohammedans, supported by the Hindu population."

Gandhi presided at the first Khalifat Conference of All India at Delhi on November 24th, 1919, and proclaimed the union of Hindus and Muslims, declaring that Hindus were at one with Mussulmans in upholding the Mussulman cause. "Already the union had been cemented in blood, when Mohammedans and Hindus were killed together by the English on the field of massacre at Amritsar."

In spite of the Muslim manifesto and deputations to London, the Peace Terms which were published on May 14th, 1920, proved to be disastrous to Turkey, and caused deep indignation among the Muslims, who decided on May 28th, 1920, to adopt Gandhi's Non-Co-operation policy. A joint Hindu-Muslim conference held at Allahabad on June 30th, 1920, unanimously adopted Non-Co-operation, giving a month's notice to the Viceroy.

Attitude of British Government

The British Government not only wakened up to the danger too late, but committed the same crimes in India that previous Governments had committed in Ireland, sandwiching microscopic concessions with macroscopic coercion.

The Montagu-Chelmsford Reforms, which we deal with elsewhere, were accompanied by a proclamation from the King on December 24th, 1919, inviting Indians to co-operate in working them, and asking the Viceroy to amnesty political prisoners.

Although he judged the reforms inadequate and incomplete, Gandhi considered them and the proclamation together as an olive branch, as an offer of peace, and counselled their acceptance by the National Congress, which otherwise, in all probability, would have rejected them, for many of the leaders looked upon them as a trap.

Later Gandhi changed his views on the subject, and recognised that he had walked into a trap.

His hopes of peace and justice were soon dashed by the Viceroy, who, instead of showing clemency according to the King's request, permitted many political prisoners to languish in gaols, and some to be sent to execution, a *dénouement* which broke Indian confidence in British good faith.

Non-Co-operation

The programme of Non-Co-operation drawn up by Gandhi and his committee of Non-Co-operators included :—

1. Surrender of titles and honorary offices.
2. Non-participation in Government loans.
3. Refusal to attend Government levées, durbars, etc.
4. Boycott of schools and colleges controlled by the Government.
5. Boycott of British courts and settlement of disputes by private arbitration.
6. Boycott of reformed councils.
7. Refusal on the part of military, clerical and labouring classes to recruit the services in Mesopotamia.
8. The propagation of Swadeshi, of spinning and weaving in every home, with the boycott of foreign cloth.

9. Removal of "untouchability."
10. Removal of drink curse.

In his own words, Gandhi said, "Personally I do not mind Governmental fury as I mind mob fury," and accordingly he took precautions to keep order and discipline in the ranks of Non-Co-operators, maintaining that "effective Non-Co-operation depends upon complete organisation, and disorderliness comes from anger, orderliness out of intelligent resistance; . . . that the first condition of real success is to ensure entire absence of violence; . . . that violence done to persons representing the Government or to persons who don't join our ranks means retrogression, cessation of Non-Co-operation, and useless waste of innocent lives."

European revolutionists rub their eyes in astonishment when they read this programme and advocacy of non-violence, and wonder what good thing can come out of it in the way of freedom, forgetting that Non-Co-operation had been tried in other countries, like Hungary and Ireland, and had finally succeeded.

On August 1st, 1920, Mahatma Gandhi inaugurated the Non-Co-operative Movement by returning his titles and decorations in a famous letter to the Viceroy: "It is not without a pang that I return the Kaisar-i-Hind gold medal granted to me by your predecessor for my humanitarian work in South Africa, the Zulu War medal granted in South Africa for my services as officer-in-charge of the Indian Volunteer Ambulance Corps in 1906, and the Boer War medal for my services as assistant superintendent of the Indian Volunteer Stretcher-Bearer Corps during the Boer War of 1899–1900. I venture to return these medals in pursuance of the scheme of Non-Co-operation. Valuable as these honours have been to me, I cannot wear them with an easy conscience so long as my Mussulman countrymen have to labour under a wrong done to their religious sentiments. Events that have happened during the past month have confirmed me in the opinion that the Imperial Government have acted in the Khalifat matter in an unscrupulous, immoral and unjust manner, and have been moving from wrong to wrong in order to defend their immorality. I can retain neither respect nor affection for such a Government.

"The attitude of the Imperial and Your Excellency's Government in the Punjab question has given me additional cause for grave dissatisfaction. I had the honour as one of the Congress Commissioners to investigate the causes of the disorders in the Punjab during April, 1919. And it is my deliberate conviction that Sir Michael O'Dwyer was totally unfit to hold the office of Lieutenant-Governor of Punjab, and that his policy was primarily responsible for infuriating the mob at Amritsar. No doubt the mob excesses were unpardonable; incendiarism, murder of five innocent Englishmen, and the cowardly assault on Miss Sherwood were most deplorable and uncalled for. But the preventive measures taken by General Dyer and other officers were out of all proportion to the crime of the people, and amounted to wanton cruelty and inhumanity almost unparalleled in modern times.

"Your Excellency's light-hearted treatment of the official crime, your exoneration of Sir Michael O'Dwyer, Mr. Montagu's despatch, and, above all, the shameful ignorance of the Punjab events and callous disregard of the feelings of Indians betrayed by the House of Lords, have filled me with the gravest misgivings regarding the future of the Empire, have estranged me completely from the present Government, and have disabled me from tendering, as I have hitherto whole-heartedly tendered, my loyal co-operation.

"In my humble opinion the ordinary method of agitating by way of petitions, deputations, and the like is no remedy for moving to repentance a Government so hopelessly indifferent to the welfare of its charge as the Government of India has proved to be. In European countries, condemnation of such grievous wrongs as the Khalifat and the Punjab would have resulted in a bloody revolution by the people. They would have resisted at all cost national emasculation such as the said wrongs imply. But half of India is too weak to offer such violent resistance, and the other half is unwilling to do so. I have, therefore, ventured to suggest the remedy of Non-Co-operation, which enables those who wish to to disassociate themselves from the Government, and which, if it is unattended by violence and undertaken in an ordered manner, must compel it to retrace its steps and undo the wrongs committed. But whilst I shall pursue the policy of Non-Co-operation in so far as I can carry the people with me, I shall not lose hope that you will yet see your way to do justice. I, therefore, respectfully ask Your Excellency to summon a conference of the recognised leaders of the people, and in consultation with them find a way that would placate the Mussulmans and do reparation to the unhappy Punjab."

Gandhi's example was followed at once by hundreds of magistrates resigning, by abandonment of the law courts, by withdrawal of thousands of students from schools and colleges, and Indian universities, Indian colleges and schools, free from Government control, springing up in their place.

A special session of the Indian National Congress was held at Calcutta in September, which sanctioned Gandhi's programme and decided that non-violent Non-Co-operation must be adopted until India's wrongs were righted and Swaraj (Home Rule) was established.

Mahatma Gandhi, Maulana Mohammad Ali, and others toured through the country, amidst scenes of wild enthusiasm, conducting a campaign at the same time to advance Hindu-Muslim unity, the settlement of disputes between Brahmins and non-Brahmins, and to rid Hinduism of the reproach of "untouchability."

To a friendly critic, who deplored "direct action" and appealed to Gandhi as a "saint" to take up the larger mission of uniting the world, the Mahatma's reply is worth reading *in extenso* in *Young India* of May 12th, 1920, but the following extracts reveal the character of our hero: "The word 'saint' should be ruled out of present life. It is too sacred a word to be lightly applied to anybody, much less to one, like myself, who claims only to be a humble searcher after truth. . . . The politician in me has never dominated a single decision of mine, and if I seem to take part in politics, it is only because politics encircle us to-day like the coil of a snake from which one cannot get out, no matter how one tries. . . . Never has anything been done on this earth without "direct action." It was direct action in South Africa which converted General Smuts. I rejected the word 'passive resistance' because of its insufficiency. . . . What was the larger 'symbiosis' that Buddha and Christ preached? Buddha fearlessly carried the war into the enemy's camp and brought down on its knees an arrogant priesthood. Christ drove out the money-changers from the temple of Jerusalem, and drew down curses from Heaven upon the hypocrites and the Pharisees. Both were intensely for direct action. But even as Buddha and Christ chastised, they showed unmistakable gentleness and love behind every act of theirs. . . . Christ died on the cross with a crown of thorns on his head defying the might of a whole empire. And if I raise resistances of a non-violent character, I simply and humbly follow in the footsteps of the great teachers."

Romain Rolland emphasised the fact that Gandhi's campaign had not only for object the paralysing of the English Government by Non-Co-operation, but the organisation of a new India capable of supporting herself, and of creating her material and moral independence. Towards national and economic independence Swadeshi was the sanest and simplest means in Gandhi's opinion (an opinion from which he has never swerved in spite of any amount of criticism), and which he summed up as follows : " (1) Learn spinning yourself, whether man or woman. Charge for the labour if you need money, or make a gift of at least an hour's labour to the nation daily. (2) Learn weaving yourself, whether for recreation or for maintenance. (3) Make improvements in the present handlooms and the spinning wheels, and if you are rich pay for them to those who would make them. (4) Take the Swadeshi vow and patronise the cloth that is both hand-spun and hand-woven. (5) Introduce such cloth among your friends, and believe that there is more art and humanity in Khadi whose yarn has been prepared by your poor sisters. (6) If you are a mother, you will give a clean and national culture to your children and make them wear clothes made out of beautiful Khadi, which is available to millions and which can be most easily produced. Swadeshi involves the honour of Indian womanhood. It will save them from road labour and from working in the mills. It means even distribution of wealth from an occupation next in importance only to agriculture. It supplements agriculture, and, therefore, automatically assists nationally to solve the problem of our growing poverty. It will help to save the annual drain of 60 million rupees."

Towards moral independence it would be necessary to deny themselves many national satisfactions, to practise and obey laws of health, above all, to root out "the curse of drink" and to boycott the wines of Europe. So strong was the wave of temperance that the Mahatma was compelled to intervene and stop the crowds from closing the drink-shops by force or from sacking them, when he explained that "It is not permissible to make people pure by force."

The music of the spinning wheel, of the Charkha, whose every revolution spins peace, goodwill and love, excited the benediction of India's venerable national poet, Rabindranath Tagore, who had already relinquished his title from patriotic motives.

When Gandhi gave the order to burn foreign manufactured clothes, which he regarded as an emblem of slavery, and Bombay consigned to the flames in August, 1921, a pyramid of the finest sadis, shirts and jackets, to the tumultuous joy of a vast concourse of people, who felt that their shackles were being broken, Mr. C. F. Andrews, one of the firmest friends of India, one who wore Khaddar, and one of the greatest admirers of the Mahatma, protested that it shocked him, because he feared that it was a form almost of violence, a subtle appeal to racial feeling, a retrograde step to the old, bad, selfish nationalism. "I was supremely happy when you were dealing great giant blows at the great fundamental moral evils, drunkenness, drug-taking, untouchability, race arrogance, etc., and when you were, with such wonderful and beautiful tenderness, dealing with the hideous vice of prostitution. But lighting bonfires of foreign cloth and telling people it is a religious sin to wear it—. . . I cannot tell you how different all this appears to me." Thus wrote Andrews to his friend Gandhi, who replied, in a loving spirit, on the "Ethics of Destruction," from which I cull the following quotations: "I remain just as convinced as ever of the necessity of burning. There is no emphasis on the process of race feeling. . . . Experience shows that the richest gifts must be destroyed without compensation and hesitation, if they hinder one's moral progress. . . . If the emphasis were on all foreign things, it would be racial, parochial and wicked. The emphasis is on all foreign cloth. The restriction makes all the difference in the world. I do not want to shut out English lever watches or the beautiful Japanese lacquer work. Love of foreign cloth has brought foreign domination, pauperism, and, what is worst, shame to many a home. . . . Not long ago hundreds of 'instructible' weavers of Kathiawar, having found their calling gone, became sweepers. And some are helpless witnesses of the shame of their daughters and even their wives, who, under pressure of one sort or another, are obliged to sell their honour. . . . Proud weavers of the Punjab, for want of occupation, not many years ago, took to the sword and were instructed in killing the proud and innocent Arabs at the bidding of their officers, and not for the sake of this country but for the sake of their livelihood. . . . Is it now any wonder, if I consider it a sin to touch foreign cloth? . . . Foreign cloth to India is like foreign matter to the body. The destruction of the former is as necessary for the health of India as of the latter for the health of the body. . . . India is to-day nothing but a dead mass movable at the will of another. Let her become alive by self-purification, *i.e.*, self-restraint and self-denial, and she will be a boon to herself and mankind. Let her be carelessly self-indulgent, aggressive, grasping, and if she rises, she will do so like Kumbha Karma, only to destroy and be a curse to herself and mankind."

"On the racial, parochial and wicked" side of the argument Mahatma Gandhi might effectively have quoted the action of the British Government, which stamps all letters sent through the Post Office in bold letters, big enough for the blind to read, with "Buy British Goods," "British Goods are Best."

Gandhi argued that millions of Indians had been ruined by English manufactures; that many had fallen to the rank of pariahs and mercenary soldiers, and their wives and daughters to prostitution; that Indians hated their English exploiters, and, therefore, the hatred must be turned from men to things. He did not hesitate to lay the blame on the Indians who bought as well as on the English who sold. With him the consuming of foreign cloth in bonfires was a necessary surgical operation, performed not as an act of hatred, but of repentance. To have given these soiled goods to the poor, as suggested by some, would, in his view, have been dishonourable.

Recognising that economic freedom would be foolish without spiritual freedom, Mahatma Gandhi was anxious to substitute Indian culture for European, and to that end he opened the National University of Gujerat at Ahmedabad in November, 1920. On that occasion he unfolded some of his ideals: "The National University stands to-day as a protest against British injustice, and as a vindication of national honour. . . . It draws its inspiration from the national ideals of a united India. It stands for a religion which is the Dharma of the Hindus and Islam of Mohammedans. It wants to rescue the Indian vernaculars from unmerited oblivion and make them the foundations of national regeneration and Indian culture. It holds that a systematic study of Asiatic cultures is no less essential than the study of Western sciences for a complete education for life. The vast treasures of Sanskrit and Arabic, Persian and Pali, and Magadhi have to be ransacked in order to discover wherein lies the source of strength for the nation. It does not propose merely to feed on or repeat the ancient cultures. It rather hopes to build a new culture based on the traditions of the past, enriched by the experience of later times. It stands for the synthesis of the different cultures that have come to stay in India, that have influenced Indian life, and that, in their turn, have themselves been influenced by the spirit of the soil. This synthesis will naturally be of the Swadeshi type, where each culture is assured its legitimate place, and not of American pattern, where one dominant culture absorbs the rest, and where the aim is not towards harmony, but towards an artificial and forced unity. That is why the University has desired a study of all the Indian religions by its students. The Hindus may thus have an opportunity of studying the Koran, and the Muslims of knowing what the Hindu Shastras contain. If the University has excluded anything, it is the spirit of exclusion that regards any section of humanity as permanently untouchable. The study of Hindustani, which is a national blend of

Sanskrit, Hindu and Persianised Urdu, has been made compulsory. The spirit of independence will be fostered, not only through religion, politics, and history, but through vocational training also, which can give the youths of the country economic independence and a backbone that comes out of a sense of self-respect. The University hopes to organise higher schools throughout the mofussil towns, so that education may be spread broadcast and filtered down to the masses as early as possible. The use of Gujerati as the medium of education will facilitate this process, and ere long the suicidal cleavage between the educated and non-educated will be bridged. And, as an effect of industrial education to the genteel folks and literary education for the industrial classes, the unequal distribution of wealth and the consequent social discontent will be considerably checked. The greatest defect of the Government universities has been their alien control and the false values they have created as regards 'careers.' The Gujerati University, by non-co-operating with the Government, has automatically eradicated both these evils from its own system. If the founders and promoters stick to this resolve till the Government becomes nationalised, it will help them to cultivate a clear perception of national ideals and national needs."

This long quotation is given for the purpose of enabling the reader to know the man who defied British authority in India.

To rear educators for the young, Gandhi established a monastery at Ahmedabad—Satyagrah Ashram—where masters and pupils subscribed to the vows of—(1) truth, never to lie even for the benefit of their country; (2) Ahimsa, not to kill even tyrants, but to conquer by love; (3) celibacy; (4) simpler living;

(5) not to steal, a theft being defined as the employment of objects of which we have no real need ; (6) non-possession of everything which is not absolutely necessary for the body's requirements ; (7) Swadeshi, boycott of foreign goods and clothes ; (8) fearlessness, freedom from fear of kings, people, family, men, wild beasts, and death. At the end of ten years' training these young servants of India had a free choice to take these vows or retire.

Romain Rolland describes this spiritual work of Mahatma Gandhi as the creation of a legion of apostles who, like those of Christ, would be the salt of the earth, and he designates the Mahatma as the moulder of a new humanity.

How richly the Mahatma deserved this high esteem of the great French writer may be appreciated by the reader when he learns that during the stern and strenuous fight against the British Government Gandhi combined the combat for the rights of man with the combat for the rights of nations, the rights of the oppressed classes in India with the rights of India to complete justice and equality in the brotherhood of men and of nations. " If Indians," he argued, " have become pariahs of the Empire, it is the return of eternal justice. . . . Untouchability has degraded India. Even the Mussalmans caught the sinful contagion from us, and in South Africa, in East Africa and in Canada, the Mussalmans, no less than Hindus, came to be regarded as pariahs. All this evil has resulted from the sin of untouchability. . . The first duty is to protect the weak, and not to outrage the human conscience. We are no better than brutes as long as we fail to wash ourselves of this sin. Swaraj ought to be the reign of justice on earth." He was prepared even to sacrifice his religion if untouchability formed part of its dogma. He presided over the "Suppressed Classes Conference" at Ahmedabad in April, 1921. He organised them, and on his initiation the Indian National Congress passed the resolution stating that the removal of this blot on Hinduism was necessary for the attainment of Swaraj.

The cause of women, their emancipation from social and political injustice, from the curse of early marriage and from the degrading evils of prostitution, never had a nobler, more devoted, and more powerful champion than Mahatma Gandhi.

In the words of Rolland, Gandhi succeeded in harmonising religion, patriotism and humanity. What more can we say of this light of the world, of this bright effluence of bright essence increate, of this prince of peace, of this beautiful reflection or reincarnation of Buddha and Christ?

BRITISH REPRESSION OF NON-CO-OPERATION

At first the Viceroy, Lord Chelmsford, treated the Non-Co-operative Movement with superior contempt, saying in August, 1920, that "of all the foolish schemes this was the most foolish," but by November 6th of the same year he issued an official statement threatening to institute criminal proceedings against those who passed the limits of non-violence. The limits were soon passed, but by the Government, as Rolland points out.

In December, 1920, the Indian National Congress at Nagpur, at which there were 469 Mussulmans, 65 Sikhs, 5 Parsis, 2 untouchables, 106 women, and 4,079 Hindus, as delegates, confirmed (instead of rejected, as the Government hoped) the Non-Co-operation vote of the special session in September, inscribing as the first article of its constitution :—

"The object of the National Congress is to attain Swaraj for the people of India by every pacific and legitimate means."

Further, the Congress announced that refusal to pay taxes would be resorted to if necessary. Meanwhile all Indians were exhorted to practise with more zeal the programme of Non-Co-operation. This was regarded by the British bureaucracy as an affirmation of a State within the State, of an Indian State against the British Government, and instead of seeking an understanding with the Indian leaders of the patriotic movement in a conciliatory spirit, the British authorities determined to destroy Indian nationalism by repression and violence, the usual weapons employed by Imperialists in treating with subject races.

Curiously enough, the outbreaks of violence on the part of the Government occurred in extraneous movements, when the police put down with bloodshed an agarian revolt of tenants against landlords in the United Provinces. Next, the Government intervened in the Akali agitation in the Punjab amongst the Sikhs, who sought to reform and control their religious shrines, and in February, 1921, the Government failed to prevent the massacre of unarmed and devotedly religious Sikhs, when 200 men were killed, and more wounded, by the partisans of the Mahants, whose claims to certain temples Government supported.

With regard to the Akali movement, the writer feels it to be his duty to place on record that when he visited Lahore in January, 1926, he found large numbers of Sikhs still in gaols, undergoing sentences for a religious strike, the justice of which strike was practically acknowledged by the Gurdwara Act, recently passed by the Legislative Council of the Punjab, and accepted by the Punjab Government, by which the shrines are restored to the Sikhs. So deeply was I stirred that I made a public appeal to the Governor of the Province to release these prisoners, not merely as an act of conciliation and grace, but as an act of justice. I believe that they have been released since.

The Government then resorted to repression of the Non-Co-operators, culminating in the suppression of volunteer organisations, the promulgation of the Seditious Meetings Act, and the arrest and incarceration of thousands of Indians on mere suspicion. For the benefit of the reader, it should be explained that "sedition" is an extraordinarily comprehensive offence in the eyes of the Government of India, including the preaching of "disaffection" to the Government, a crime which is committed in England (and wherever parliamentary government exists) by every political party when in opposition, whether it be Liberal, Labour or Tory.

Volunteers by the hundreds were thrown into gaols for "peaceful picketing" of liquor shops, which formed an important source of revenue to the Government, and the picketing of which the Government would not tolerate, preferring India drunk to India sober, and India immoral to India pure. This was not the first time that alcoholism and European civilisation marched together, remarks Rolland. *Carte-blanche* was given to the police to crush the movement, and coercion produced reprisals, collisions between the mob and the police, and murders and incendiarism, just as happened in Ireland when the British Government gave way to lawlessness.

With the growth of the national movement the "brutal repressions"—Rolland's description—and immorality of the Government increased beyond all bounds. Riots, accompanied by bloodshed, burst out at Malegaon, in Nasik, at Giridih, in Berar, and elsewhere, but worse was to follow. In May, 1921, 12,000 coolies working in the tea-gardens of Assam struck on account of low wages, and made a great exodus to Chanpur, where they were attacked by Gurkhas in the service of the Government. To the exquisite torture of starvation were added the horrors of militarism by a British Government professing paternal friendship and trusteeship for the poor. This display of frightfulness led to a sympathetic strike among the working classes on the railroads and steamers in East Bengal, which created a complete deadlock for nearly two months.

Becoming alarmed or conscience-stricken, Lord Reading, the Viceroy, had long interviews with Mahatma Gandhi, Lala Lajpat Rai, and Pandit Madan Mohan Malaviya, but without relaxing his policy of coercion and tyranny, and without exhibiting any trace of statesmanship by removing the causes of the national disorders of his own, his predecessor's and the Home Government's creation. The Ali brothers, the stout leaders of the Muslims, had been accused of speeches calculated to provoke violence; Gandhi obtained from his Mussulman friends a formal declaration that they would never appeal to violence.

The Khalifat Conference of All India, which met at Karachi on July 8th, 1921, reiterated the demands of Islam, and passed a resolution declaring it "unlawful for any faithful Mussulman to serve from that day in the army or help or acquiesce in the recruitment." It also declared that, if the British Government fought the Angora Government, the Muslims of India would start civil disobedience and hoist the flag of the Indian Republic.

The All India Congress Committee meeting at Bombay on July 28th resolved to boycott the Prince of Wales, because it regarded the visit of the Prince as a "political move" calculated to give strength and support to a system of government that has resulted in a breach of faith with the Mussulmans and atrocious injustice to the people of India, and a system that is designed to keep India as long as possible from her birthright of Swaraj. This was the first meeting of the committee after the inauguration of the deceptive reforms.

On August 19th the Moplahs (a Mussulman community) of Malabar broke out into open rebellion, at first against the Government, but subsequently against the Hindu population as well. The immediate cause of the outbreak was the attempted arrest by the District Magistrate of some Khalifat workers, following on ruthless repression of their legitimate activities. Carried away by fanaticism and ignorance, these wild men looted Hindu houses, forcibly converted some of the inhabitants, and committed unmentionable atrocities. They received short shrift at the hands of the military, and sometimes slow and painful death. On one occasion they were herded together like cattle in tightly closed trucks on the railway, and died from asphyxiation without their cries for water being heard; seventy were taken out dead at the end of a day's journey. The Mahatma and Maulana Mahomed Ali hurried from Calcutta to Malabar to pacify the Moplahs, but were prevented by the Government in their mission of peace.

In September fear took possession of the Government, and the leading Muslims, Mahomed Ali, Shaukat Ali, Dr. Kitchlew, Pir Galam Mujadid, Nisar Ahmed, etc., were arrested for the proposals of civil disobedience voted at the Khalifat Conference. Gandhi at once took up the cudgels on behalf of his brother-Mussulmans, and published a manifesto, signed by fifty eminent members of the National Congress, vindicating the right of every citizen to express his opinion upon non-participation with a Government which has caused the moral, economic and political degradation of India.

The Ali brothers were brought to trial at Karachi, and, along with their comrades, sentenced to two years' rigorous imprisonment.

The Committee of the National Congress met at Delhi on November 4th, and, after confirming Gandhi's manifesto, took the decisive step of authorising civil disobedience by the non-payment of taxes, imposing the conditions of the programme of Swadeshi and of Non-Co-operation, and emphasising non-violence.

On November 17th the Prince of Wales landed in Bombay, where he was received by officials, Europeans, Parsis and the rich, but boycotted by the middle and working classes. Mobs got out of hand and began to molest visitors to the reception. From small beginnings the riots assumed larger proportions ; tramcars were burnt, liquor shops smashed, and even some Parsi ladies molested. Mahatma Gandhi, who also happened to be in Bombay, holding a meeting in another part of the city, rushed to the scene, censured the crowds and implored them to disperse. He said that the Parsis had the right to welcome the Prince if they wished, and that nothing could excuse unworthy violence. At first his appeal succeeded, but later the unruly elements broke loose again, and many persons were wounded and killed during the next few days. Romain Rolland remarks that the riots remained limited all the time; the least of our revolutionary days in Europe would leave more damage. This was the only brutal explosion in all India, where the *hartal* (the solemn strike) was religiously observed in peace, without incidents.

Gandhi, however, was " pierced as by an arrow," and publicly declared that such misdoings rendered impossible mass civil disobedience, which he suspended. To punish himself for the violence of others he imposed upon himself a religious fast of twenty-four hours every week.

After the Bombay riots panic seized the Europeans in India, who pressed the Viceroy to take immediate action, which he did by declaring, on November 19th, the Khalifat and Congress Volunteer Corps unlawful under section 16 of the Indian Criminal Law Amendment Act, 1908, which had been passed to suppress anarchists and secret societies. Thousands of arrests of innocent Indians were made, and the Europeans, who in their cups and in their clubs stigmatise Indians as cowardly, breathed again freely.

One must not be too severe or too caustic in criticism of the Viceroy, for he only did what Imperialists have always done in similar circumstances, what the Russian Czarists did in Poland, what the Austrians did in Italy, and what the British did in Ireland. Another reflection on his action which naturally arises is his sensitiveness to the opinion of the English residents in India, and his utter disregard of the opinion of Indians, on whose behalf he was supposed to govern India. His behaviour as well as that of his predecessor, Lord Chelmsford, in the reign of terror which they conducted against

Indians rightly struggling to be free, is another proof of the impossibility of one nation to govern another righteously. In the long and tragic history of Imperialism, no nation has ever succeeded in ruling another without gross and disastrous injury and injustice. Will the English people learn this simple truth, and, learning it, hand over the government of India to Indians, who by nature are best fitted to govern themselves ?

The reign of terror and coercion proceeded according to plan by the Government arresting and imprisoning, in the beginning of December, the leaders of Indian nationalism for no baser crime than loving their country, for working zealously and constitutionally for its emancipation from British domination. Mr. C. R. Das, the next-best-beloved man to Gandhi in India, Pandit Motilal Nehru, the highly venerated legal luminary, Lala Lajpat Rai, the lion of the Punjab, Maulana Abul Kalam Azad, the heroic Mussulman, were pitched into gaols, as if they were the scum of the earth, along with thousands of young volunteers who differed from Lord Birkenhead, Lord Carson, Mr. Bonar Law, and other Tory revolutionaries, in that they pledged themselves to non-violence. Indian national sentiment was outraged, and the Moderates protested strongly against this violent attack on the elementary rights of citizens, sending a deputation under Madan Mohase Malruja to the Viceroy to request the withdrawal of the notification under the Criminal Law Amendment Act and the Seditious Meetings Act and the release of the persons imprisoned under them, and also the calling of a Round Table Conference of the representatives of the people to solve and discuss with the Government the problem of India's freedom. The Viceroy rejected the offer of "peace with honour," hardened his heart against

Indians like Pharaoh did against the Israelites, and plunged deeper into repression.

Meanwhile the Prince of Wales was subjected to the foolish and provocative policy of the Viceroy, to the humiliation of marching through the streets of Calcutta bristling with bayonets, but deserted by the populace, on December 24th, which day was observed by Indians as a complete *hartal*. How much longer is the Home Government going to abuse the Prince by making him a "commercial traveller" and "smoother" of Imperial mistakes? It is not only dishonouring to him, but dishonouring to our country, and tends to strengthen the growing conviction in India and in the world that the Indian Empire is run and retained for profits.

The illustrious Frenchman, author of "Gandhi," seemed to find a parallel between the Indian National Congress, which opened at Ahmedabad at this time, and the Etats Généraux of 1789. The President (C. R. Das) was incarcerated. The discussions were brief. The principle of Non-Co-operation reaffirmed; all citizens were invoked to offer themselves as "volunteers," in order to be arrested; the people were invited to hold public meetings everywhere; "civil disobedience" was proclaimed equal in force and superior in humanitarianism to "armed rebellion;" and as soon as the masses were initiated into the methods of non-violence civil disobedience was put into operation. Foreseeing that most of the members would be arrested at the end of the session, the Congress delegated all powers to Gandhi, a dictatorship in fact, with the right to appoint his successor, with one reserve only, that the national *credo* should not be modified, and that peace with the Government should not be concluded without the consent of the Congress Committee. A fraction of the assembled delegates moved a resolution which tended to violent action in order to establish as soon as possible the complete independence of India, but the majority rejected it in fidelity to Gandhi's principles.

India had found her soul, for 40,000 men and women went joyfully to prison for the sake of their country, and behind them thousands of others arose waiting their turn to affirm their patriotism.

Mass civil disobedience by refusal to pay taxes, Gandhi announced to the Viceroy in a courteous letter on February 8th, 1922, would be started in Bardoli, a district in the Province of Bombay, comprising 140 villages, with 87,000 inhabitants, as a protest against the Government, which had put down brutally liberty of speech, liberty of association, and liberty of the press, unless the policy of the Government was changed for the better within seven days.

Scarcely had this letter been posted than the drama of Chauri Chaura, in the district of Gorakhpur, took place. An unarmed procession was attacked by the police, who in turn were attacked by the members of the procession, upon whom the police opened fire, and, then overpowered, sought refuge in the police station, to which the population set fire, when the policemen were either burnt to death or killed by the mob.

Gandhi was torn to pieces by this tragedy, taking upon himself the sins of the people, although not one "volunteer" had participated in the crime. Having despatched his ultimatum to the Viceroy a day or two before, how could he withdraw it without ridicule? "Satan," pride, forbade him. Putting Satan behind him, he bravely stopped civil disobedience for the second time, and on February 16th, 1922, published "My Confession," one of the most extraordinary documents of his extraordinary life, from which the following extracts are taken :—

"God has been abundantly kind to me. He has warned me the third time that there is not as yet in India that truthful and non-violent atmosphere which, and which alone, can justify mass disobedience, which can be at all described as civil, which means gentle, truthful, humble, knowing, wilful yet loving, never criminal and hateful. He warned me in 1919 when the Rowlatt Act agitation was started. Ahmedabad, Viramgam and Kheda erred; Amritsar and Kasur erred. I retraced my steps, called it a Himalayan miscalculation, humbled myself before God and man, and stopped not merely mass civil disobedience, but even my own, which I know was intended to be civil and non-violent. The next time it was through the events of Bombay that God gave a terrific warning. He made me an eye-witness. . . . I stopped mass civil disobedience which was to be immediately started in Bardoli. The humiliation was greater, but it did me good. I am sure that the nation gained by the stopping. India stood for truth and non-violence. But the bitterest humiliation is that of to-day. . . . God spoke clearly through Chauri Chaura. . . . When India hopes to mount the throne of liberty through non-violence, mob violence even in answer to grave provocation is a bad augury. . . . Non-violent non-co-operators can only succeed when they have succeeded in attaining control over the hooligans of India. . . . The drastic reversal of the whole of the aggressive programme may be politically unsound and unwise, but there is no doubt that it is religiously sound, and I venture to assure the doubters that the country will have gained by my humiliation and confession of error. The only virtue I want to claim is truth and non-violence. I lay no claim to superhuman powers. I want none. I wear the same corruptible flesh that the weakest of my fellow-beings wear, and am, therefore, as liable to err as any. My services have many limitations, but God has up to now blessed them in spite of the imperfections. . . . Confession of error is like a broom that sweeps away dirt. . . . I feel stronger for my confession. And the cause must prosper for the retracing. Never has man reached his destination by persistence in deviation from the straight path. . . . It has been argued that Chauri Chaura cannot affect Bardoli. . . . I have no doubt on that account. The people of Bardoli are, in my opinion, the most peaceful in India. But Bardoli is but a speck on the map of India. Its effect cannot succeed unless there is perfect co-operation from the other parts. . . . A grain of arsenic in a pot of milk renders it unfit as food. . . . Chauri Chaura is a deadly poison, . . . and Chauri Chaura represents India as much as Bardoli. . . . *In civil disobedience there should be no excitement. Civil disobedience is a preparation for mute suffering.* . . . Its effect is marvellous, though unperceived and gentle. . . . The tragedy of Chauri Chaura is really the index finger. . . . If we are not to evolve violence out of non-violence, we must hastily retrace our steps, and re-establish an atmosphere of peace, and not think of starting mass civil disobedience until we are sure of peace being retained in spite of Government provocation. . . . Let the opponent glory in our so-called defeat. It is better to be charged with cowardice than to sin against God. . . . I must undergo personal purification. *I must become a fitter instrument, able to register the slightest variation in the moral atmosphere about me.* My prayers must have much deeper truth and humility. . . . For me there is nothing so helpful and purifying as a fast, accompanied by the necessary mental co-operation. . . . I am imposing on myself a five days' continuous fast, permitting myself water. . . . I urge co-workers not to copy my example, for they are not the originators of disobedience. . . . I have been an unskilful surgeon. I must either abdicate or acquire greater skill. . . . My fasting is both a penance and a punishment for myself and for those who sinned at Chauri Chaura. . . . I would advise those who are guilty and repentant to hand themselves voluntarily to the Government for punishment, and make a clean confession, for they have injured the very cause they intended to serve. . . . I would suffer every humiliation, every torture, absolute ostracism and death itself to prevent the movement from becoming violent or a precursor of violence."

Romain Rolland's comment on Gandhi's confession and action will interest the reader. Freely translated, it is, "The history of the human conscience counts few pages so lofty. The moral worth of such an action is exceptional. But as an act of policy it was disconcerting. Gandhi himself recognised that it might be judged 'politically absurd and unwise.' It is dangerous to unite all the resources of a people, to cry halt before the aim is achieved, to give the command to proceed and then when the formidable machine is in motion to stop it three times. It risks shattering hope."

When the All India Congress assembled at Delhi on February 24th, 1922, a vote of censure against the Bardoli decision to drop civil disobedience was submitted; but the majority supported the Mahatma, who was under no illusion as to the schism in the ranks of the Congress, which caused him great anguish. With his customary courage and frankness, he referred to it on March 2nd, 1922, in the following terms: " There was so much undercurrent of violence, both conscious and unconscious, that I was actually praying for a disastrous defeat. I have always been in a minority. . . . In South Africa I started with unanimity, reached a minority of sixty-four, and even sixteen, and went up again to a huge majority. The best and the most solid work was done in the wilderness of minority. The only thing that the Government dread is this huge majority I command. They little know that I dread it even more than they. I have become sick of the admiration of the unthinking multitude. I would feel certain of my ground if I was spat upon by them. . . . A friend warned me against exploiting my dictatorship. . . . Far from exploiting my 'dictatorship,' I have begun to wonder if I am not allowing myself to be 'exploited.' I confess that I have a dread of it such as I never had before. My only safety lies in my shamelessness. I have warned my friends of the Committee that I am incorrigible. I shall continue to confess blunders each time the people commit them. The only tyrant I accept in this world is the 'still small voice' within. And even though I have to face the prospect of a minority of one, I believe I have the courage to be in such a hopeless minority. That to me is the only truthful position. I am a sadder and, I hope, a wiser man to-day. Our non-violence is skin-deep. We are burning with indignation. The Government is feeding it by its insensate acts. It seems almost as if the Government wants to see this land covered with murder, arson and rapine, in order to be able to claim exclusive ability to put them down."

" This non-violence seems to be due merely to our

helplessness, as if we are nursing in our bosoms the desire to take revenge the first time we get the opportunity. Can voluntary non-violence come out of this forced non-violence of the weak? Is it not a futile experiment I am conducting? What if, when the fury burst, not a man, woman or child is safe, and every man's hand is raised against his fellow? Of what avail is it then, if I fast myself to death after such a catastrophe? . . . Co-operation with the Government is as much a weakness and a sin as alliance with suspended violence. . . . If it is through 'show of force' that we wish to gain Swaraj, let us drop non-violence, and offer such violence as we may. It would be a manly, honest and sober attitude—an attitude the world has been used to for ages past. No man can then accuse us of the terrible charge of hypocrisy. . . . If the majority do not believe in non-violence, let them realise their responsibility. They are now bound not to rush to civil disobedience, but to settle down to quiet work of construction. . . . If we do not take care we are likely to be drowned in the waters whose depth we do not know. . . . The minority has different ideals. It does not believe in the programme. Is it not right and patriotic for them to retire from the Congress and form a new party? . . . The country will decide which is the popular party."

It was the night in the Garden of Olives for Gandhi, as Rolland beautifully put it. He was ready to be arrested, waiting patiently in his beloved retreat, the Ashram of Sabarmati, near to Ahmedabad, amongst his devoted disciples. He had made all his dispositions "if arrested" as far back as November 10th, 1920. "I desire that the people should maintain perfect self-control, and consider the day of my arrest as a day of rejoicing. . . . If the people resort to violence, they will be playing into the hands of the Government. Their aeroplanes will then bomb the people, their Dyers will shoot into them, and their Smiths will uncover the veils of our women. There will be other officers to make the people rub their noses against the ground, crawl on their bellies, and undergo the scourge of whipping."

"In other countries Governments have been overthrown by sheer brute force, but I have often shown that India cannot attain Swaraj by that force. . . . The people should pursue peace, should not observe *hartals* (suspension of work), should not hold meetings, but carry out the programme of Non-Co-operation by vacating Government schools and opening national schools and colleges, by settlement by arbitration of cases before the law courts, by renunciation of foreign cloth, by not enlisting in the army or in any other Government service, by those able to earn their livelihood by other means withdrawing from Government services, by complete boycott of the Reformed Councils, etc. . . . If the people act thus, victory will be theirs; if not, they will be crushed."

On the evening of March 10th, a little after the hour of prayer, the police who had given previous notice arrived at Ashram, and the Mahatma delivered himself into their hands.

The great trial of Mahatma Gandhi and Mr. Banker, the printer and publisher of *Young India*, took place on March 18th before Mr. C. N. Brownsfield, District and Sessions Judge of Ahmedabad, on a charge of exciting "disaffection" towards His Majesty's Government established in British India, when both the accused pleaded guilty.

The statement made by the Mahatma on this occasion seems to me of such supreme importance for a proper understanding of the Indian view of British domination in India, that I reproduce much of it :—

" I owe it to the Indian public and to the public in England, to placate which this prosecution is mainly taken up, that I should explain why from a staunch loyalist and co-operator I have become an uncompromising disaffectionist and non-co-operator. To the court, too, I should say why I plead guilty to the charge of promoting disaffection towards the Government in India. . . . My first contact with British authority began in 1893 in South Africa, where I discovered that I had no rights as a man, because I was an Indian. . . . I thought that this treatment of Indians was an excrescence upon a system that was mainly good. I gave the Government my hearty co-operation, criticising it when I felt it was faulty, but never wishing its destruction. . . . When the Empire was threatened in 1889 by the Boer challenge, I raised a volunteer ambulance corps, . . . and similarly in 1906 in the Zulu 'rebellion.' . . . For these services I was given a Kaisar-i-Hind gold medal by Lord Hardinge. . . . In the war between England and Germany my ambulance and recruiting work was acknowledged by the authorities to be valuable. . . . In all these efforts I was actuated by the belief that it was possible by such services to gain a status of full equality in the Empire for my countrymen. The first shock came in the Rowlatt Act, a law designed to rob the people of all freedom. . . . Then followed the Punjab horrors, beginning with the massacre at Jallianwala Bagh and culminating in crawling orders, public floggings and other indescribable humiliations. . . .

"I discovered that the plighted word of the Prime Minister to the Mussulmans of India regarding the integrity of Turkey and the holy places of Islam was not likely to be fulfilled. . . . In spite of these forebodings, I fought for co-operation and working the reforms, hoping that the Prime Minister would redeem his promise, and that the Punjab wound would be healed. . . . All that hope was shattered. The promise was not to be redeemed. The Punjab crime was whitewashed, and most culprits went not to imprisonment, but remained in service, and continued to draw pensions from the Indian revenue, and some were even rewarded. I saw, too, that not only did the reforms not mark a change of heart, but they were a method of further draining India of her wealth and of prolonging her servitude. I came to the conclusion that the British connection had made India more helpless than she even was before politically and economically. A disarmed India has no power of resistance. . . . She has become so poor that she has little power of resisting famines. Before the British advent India spun and wove in her millions of cottages the supplement she needed for adding to her meagre agricultural resources. This cottage industry, so vital for India's existence, has been ruined by heartless and inhuman processes. . . . The semi-starved masses of India are slowly sinking to lifelessness. . . Their miserable condition represents the brokerage they get for the work they do for the foreign exploiter, whose profits and brokerage are sucked from the masses. . . . The government in British India is carried on for this exploitation of the masses. No sophistry, no juggling in figures, can explain away the skeletons in many villages. . . . Both England and the town-dweller of

India will have to answer, if there is a God above, for this crime against humanity, which is perhaps unequalled in history. The law itself has been used to serve the foreign exploiter. My unbiassed examination of the Punjab Martial Law cases has led me to the conclusion that in nine out of every ten the condemned men were totally innocent. Their crime consisted in the love of their country. In 99 cases out of 100 justice has been denied to Indians as against Europeans in the courts of India. . . . The greatest misfortune is that Englishmen and their Indian associates in the administration of the country do not know that they are engaged in the crime I have described. . . . Many Englishmen and Indian officials believe that they are administering one of the best systems, . . . and that India is making steady progress. . . . They do not know that a system of terrorism and an organised display of force on the one hand and the deprivation of all powers of retaliation or self-defence on the other have emasculated the people, and induced in them the habit of simulation. . . . Section 124A, under which I am charged, is designed to suppress the liberty of the citizen. Affection cannot be regulated or manufactured by law. If one has no affection for a system, one should be free to give the fullest expression to his disaffection so long as he does not incite to violence. . . . The section under which we are charged is one under which mere promotion of disaffection is a crime. . . . Some of the most loved of India's patriots have been convicted under it. I have no ill-will against any administration; much less can I have any disaffection towards the King. But I hold it to be a virtue to be disaffected towards a Government which has done more harm to India than any previous system. India is less manly under British rule than she ever was before. . . . I believe that I have rendered a service to India and England by showing in non-co-operation the way out of the unnatural state in which both are living. Non-co-operation with evil is as much a duty as co-operation with good. In the past non-co-operation has been expressed in violence to the evildoer. I am endeavouring to show to my countrymen that violent non-co-operation only multiplies evil. . . . I am here to submit cheerfully to the highest penalty that can be inflicted upon me for what in law is a crime and what appears to me to be the highest duty of a citizen. The only course open to you, the judge, is either to resign your post, if you consider the law is an evil, or to inflict on me the severest penalty, if you believe the system and the law are good for the people of this country, and that my activity is, therefore, injurious to the public weal."

In giving judgment the judge said: "Mr. Gandhi, you have made my task easy by pleading guilty. . . . It would be impossible to ignore that, in the eyes of millions of your countrymen, you are a great patriot and a great leader. Even those who differ from you in politics look upon you as a man of high ideals and of noble and of even saintly life. . . . You have consistently preached against violence, and . . . have done much to prevent violence. . . . I am trying to balance what is due to you against what appears to be necessary in the interest of the public, and I propose in passing sentence to follow the precedent of Bal Gangadhar Tilak under the same section, namely, six years' simple imprisonment; . . . and if the Government reduce the period and release you, no one will be better pleased than I."

When Tilak and Gandhi, the two noblest and most beloved citizens of India, are sentenced to six years' imprisonment for constitutionally striving for Home Rule; when the noblest and most beloved leaders of the Mohammedans are incarcerated for agitating for Home Rule; when 40,000 of India's most distinguished and cherished patriots are put in gaol for advocating Home Rule; when others without a blemish on their character are confined behind prison walls and barred doors *without charge or trial;* when love of country becomes a criminal offence, is it not time that we recognised that we have created in India a Greater Ireland, and that the solution of India's ills is Home Rule?

From March till December Gandhi's body languished in prison, in spite of the calmness and brightness of his spirit. In December he was seized with abdominal pain accompanied by fever, to which the prison officials paid little heed at first. Then becoming alarmed lest he should die on their hands, and the whole of India rise in revolt, the officials urgently called Colonel Maddock, the civil surgeon, in consultation, who diagnosed acute appendicitis, and who, without waiting for the necessary authorisation, immediately carried his patient in his car to the hospital in the neighbouring city of Poona, where he operated the same evening—January 12th—and found a deep-seated abscess attached to the appendix. The surgeon was just in time to save the patient's life, and Gandhi's gratitude to him for his kindness and skill knew no bounds.

January 18th was observed as a day of national prayer throughout India for the recovery of the national hero, and the Government was besought on all hands to release him, and the order for his discharge was signed on February 4th, 1923.

Thus endeth the second chapter of the Mahatma's work for his country. The first chapter, as we have seen, ended in a great victory for his fellow-countrymen in South Africa ; the second chapter ended, according to his enemies, British Imperialists, in failure, to which conclusion even some of his bellicose friends in the National Congress subscribed. As Mr. Lloyd George would say, he failed " to deliver the goods " : he failed to deliver India from the British yoke. Some day some historian, writing in " How India Fought for Freedom," with more enlightenment and longer vision than imperial weathercocks, will relate that Gandhi won a great moral victory over the British Empire ; that he showed to the world that Indian civilisation, with the gospel of non-violence, sacrifice and peace, is higher than British civilisation, with its doctrine of the sword, might is right, and exploitation of weak nations by physically stronger nations ; that he awakened the soul of India from the sleep of slavery, so that it will never sink back again under foreign thraldom ; and that he influenced world opinion so strongly that the British people must react quickly to it, and grant his country the inalienable right to govern itself.

" They never fail who die
In a great cause."

But Gandhi is not dead yet. He is very much alive. He is still the " Uncrowned King of India," leading and uplifting its social and spiritual life, while co-operating wisely and faithfully with its new political leaders, as we shall see in the next chapter.

CHAPTER II

CO-OPERATION IN THE COUNCILS

WITH the removal of Mahatma Gandhi from the sphere of active politics first by imprisonment and then by ill-health, Mr. C. R. Das and Pandit Motilal Nehru became the redoubtable leaders of the Indian Nationalists, who in the special Congress held in Delhi in September, 1923, passed a resolution sanctioning "Council Entry." The Swarajists, acting on this sanction, contested the elections for the Councils in December, 1923, and won a sweeping victory over the Liberals both in the Provincial Councils and All India Legislative Assembly. They had a clear majority in the Central Provinces, and, with the Independents, they commanded a majority of votes in the Legislative Assembly and in the Provincial Council of Bengal.

The Swaraj ultimatum to the Government demanded the release of all political prisoners, the repeal of all repressive laws, the immediate establishment of autonomy in the Provincial Councils, and the summoning of a National Convention to frame the future Constitution for India. If the Government refused these demands, a policy of obstruction, on the model of the Irish party under Parnell in the House of Commons, would be adopted with a view to making government, through the Assembly and the Councils, impossible. The non-acceptance of office under the Government was religiously observed when members of the party were invited to become Ministers.

This formed a substantial change in the Non-Co-operation policy of the National Congress. Gandhi's attitude to this change was, like himself, full of magnanimity: "You will not expect from me an opinion upon the delicate question of election of members of the Congress to the Legislative Councils and to the Assembly. Although I have not changed my opinions upon the boycott of the Councils, of the Law Courts, and of the Government schools, I have not the facts which permit me to arrive at a judgment upon the modification in tactics. I do not wish to express any opinion before I have been able to discuss with my illustrious compatriots their action in recommending the cessation of the boycott of the legislative bodies."

The Mahatma and his followers were not converted to the new policy of Council Entry until Lord Reading, the Viceroy, published the Bengal Ordinance on October 25th, 1924, establishing a Star Chamber for the summary arrest and trial of persons suspected of connection with associations which, in the opinion of the Government of Bengal, were revolutionary. The arrest and incarceration of the chief executive officer of Calcutta, and other distinguished members of the Swaraj party, under this nefarious ordinance, so outraged Indian national sentiment that Gandhi, Das and Nehru issued a manifesto calling for a united front on the part of all the different groups of Nationalist workers in support of the country's cause, and in opposition to the new policy of coercion, and recommending the Congress, which was to meet soon at Belgaum, to suspend the programme of Non-Co-operation so far as the Legislatures were concerned, and to encourage home-spun cloth, Hindu-Muslim unity, and the removal of untouchability.

Mr. Das had already achieved a Hindu-Muslim Pact for Bengal which laid down a definite proportional representation in all offices for the two communities.

In June, 1925, the national cause suffered a sad and severe blow by the death of C. R. Das, when the leadership of the Swarajist party fell to Pandit Motilal Nehru.

The success of the Swarajists (Home Rulers) in the All India Legislative Assembly was evidenced (1) in the rejection of the Budget of 1924–25, which the Viceroy certified, in spite of the adverse vote, under the arbitrary powers conferred upon him by the Government of India Act, and (2) in the adoption of the following resolutions, amongst others, upon the most vital questions pertaining to the political life of India :—

I. " This Assembly, while confirming and reiterating the demand contained in the Resolution passed by it on the 18th February, 1924, recommends to the Governor-General in Council that he be pleased to take immediate steps to move His Majesty's Government to make a declaration in Parliament embodying the following fundamental changes in the present constitutional machinery and administration of India :

" (*a*) The Revenue of India and all the property vested in or arising or accruing from property or rights vested in His Majesty under the Government of India Act, 1858, or the present Act, or received by the Secretary of State in Council under any of the said Acts, shall hereafter vest in the Governor-General in Council for the purposes of the Government of India.

" (*b*) The Governor-General in Council shall be responsible to the Indian Legislature, and subject to such responsibility shall have the power to control the expenditure of the Revenues of India and make such grants and appropriations of any part of those Revenues or of any other property as is at present under the control or disposal of the Secretary of State for India in Council, save and except the following, which shall for a fixed term of years remain under the control of the Secretary of State for India:

"(i.) Expenditure on the Military Services up to a fixed limit.

"(ii.) Expenditure classed as political and foreign.

"(iii.) The payment of all debts and liabilities hitherto lawfully contracted and incurred by the Secretary of State for India in Council on account of the Government of India.

"(*c*) The Council of the Secretary of State for India shall be abolished, and the position and functions of the Secretary of State for India shall be assimilated to those of the Secretary of State for the self-governing Dominions save as otherwise provided in clause (*b*).

"(*d*) The Indian Army shall be nationalised within a reasonably short and definite period of time, and Indians shall be admitted for service in all arms of defence, and for that purpose the Governor-General and the Commander-in-Chief shall be assisted by a Minister responsible to the Assembly.

"(*e*) The Central and Provincial Legislatures shall consist entirely of members elected by constituencies on as wide a franchise as possible.

"(*f*) The principle of responsibility to the Legislature

shall be introduced in all branches of the administration of the Central Government subject to transitional reservations and residuary powers in the Governor-General in respect of control of the Military, Foreign and Political affairs for a fixed term of years :

" Provided that during the said fixed term the proposals of the Governor-General in Council for the appropriation of any revenue or moneys for military or other expenditure classified as 'Defence' shall be submitted to the vote of the Legislature, but that the Governor-General in Council shall have power, notwithstanding the vote of the Assembly, to appropriate up to a fixed maximum any sum he may consider necessary for such expenditure and in the event of a war to authorise such expenditure as may be considered necessary exceeding the maximum so fixed.

"(*g*) The present system of dyarchy in the Provinces shall be abolished and replaced by unitary and autonomous responsible Governments subject to the general control and residuary powers of the Central Government in interprovincial and all-Indian matters.

"(*h*) The Indian Legislature shall after the expiry of the fixed term of years referred to in clauses (*b*) and (*f*) have full powers to make such amendments in the constitution of India from time to time as may appear to it necessary or desirable.

"This Assembly further recommends to the Governor-General in Council that necessary steps be taken :

"(*a*) To constitute in consultation with the Legislative

Assembly a convention, round table conference or other suitable agency adequately representative of all Indian, European and Anglo-Indian interests to frame, with due regard to the interests of minorities, a detailed scheme based on the above principles, after making such inquiry as may be necessary in this behalf;

"(*b*) To place the said scheme for approval before the Legislative Assembly and submit the same to the British Parliament to be embodied in a statute."

This resolution was carried by seventy-two votes to forty-five on September 8th, 1925.

II. "That this Assembly recommends to the Governor-General in Council that he be pleased:

"(*a*) Forthwith to secure the immediate release of all political prisoners detained without trial;

"(*b*) To take steps to remove all difficulties in the way of the return to India of all Indian exiles in foreign countries who may be, or may have been, suspected of being concerned in any revolutionary or other activities regarded by the Government as prejudicial to the interests of India;

"(*c*) To bring to trial under the ordinary law of the land such persons against whom the Government think that they have sufficient evidence to go to Court."

On January 26th, 1926, fifty-three voted for this resolution and forty-five against.

The importance of the voting on these occasions stands out more prominently when it is realised that the Government has a solid block of official and nominated members of about forty.

As the Government treated the resolutions of the Assembly with contempt, the obvious deduction is that there is something rotten in the Constitution which allows the Government to carry on in direct defiance of the votes of the elected representatives of the people.

In any other country with any pretence to self-government on more or less democratic lines, the Government would have resigned in similar circumstances, and the Opposition would have been asked to form a Government.

This brings us, therefore, to an examination of the Constitution under which India is governed.

CHAPTER III

THE CONSTITUTION OF INDIA

THE Constitution of India is very complex, and requires more space for its elaboration than can be given in these pages. The student of constitutional history will find in "The Indian Constitution," by Sir Tej Bahadur Sapru, an interesting analysis and comparison with other constitutions in the British Empire.

The Crown

The powers of the Crown include the appointment of an auditor of the accounts of the Secretary of State, a High Commissioner, the Governor-General, the members of the Governor-General's Executive Council, Governors, the Chief Justices and Judges of High Courts, and Advocate-General; the approval of the Constitution of a new province and the appointment of its lieutenant-governor; the assent to enable an Act which has been certified by the Governor-General to have effect; the veto on Bills and Acts submitted to or passed by local legislatures, etc.

According to the British Constitution, these powers of the Crown are exercised upon the advice of the Minister in England.

The Secretary of State

The Secretary of State is the adviser of the Crown and the agent of the British Parliament—his salary is now on the British Estimates—and has plenary powers of superintendence, direction and control over the Government of India and its revenues and over all officers appointed and continued under the Act of 1919. Constitutionally he is not and cannot be responsible to the people of India, but to Parliament, and, unfortunately for justice and progress in India, his responsibility to Parliament is largely nominal, as India, since the days of Burke, has been treated as a subject above party politics.

I must make a very grave criticism here. Whenever any great question is removed from the clash of party controversy, it is doomed to neglect by Parliament. It was so with Ireland. Until Gladstone made Ireland the live issue between Liberals and Tories Ireland was either neglected by Parliament or, worse, was subjected to tyranny, which makes us blush with shame. My contention is that India has been cruelly neglected by Parliament, and that until the leader of one of the political parties, with the vision and courage of Gladstone, forces Indian Home Rule to the front, Parliament will continue to shirk its duties, and India will continue to be misgoverned.

The Indian Council

The Indian Council sits in London, and is composed of eight to twelve members (half of whom must have served or resided in India for at least ten years), appointed by the Secretary of State. The salaries of the members are paid out of the revenues of India. Its functions are purely advisory, and the Secretary of State goes as he pleases.

Indian opinion insists on the abolition of this Council, which is either superfluous or acts as a drag on the progress of India.

The Governor-General in Council

"The superintendence, direction and control of the civil and military Government of India is vested in the Governor-General in Council, who is required to pay due obedience to all such orders as he may receive from the Secretary of State." In Lord Curzon's words, the Government of India (from the constitutional point of view) is a "subordinate branch of the British Government 6,000 miles away." But in practice it resolves itself into a question of relativity, the strong man overcoming the weaker man. With Montagu as Secretary of State and Chelmsford as Governor-General, Chelmsford was the Government of India; with Olivier as Secretary of State and Reading as Governor-General, Reading was the Government of India; and with Birkenhead as Secretary of State and Reading as Governor-General, the former was the Governor of India. Other things being equal, the odds are in favour of the "man on the spot."

The Governor-General is appointed for five years, which term was extended in the case of Lord Curzon.

His Council consists of eight members, appointed by the Crown, and their term of office is customarily five years. The Commander-in-Chief of the Army is an extraordinary member. The Governors of Madras and Bombay become extraordinary members of the Council when it meets within their presidencies.

As three at least of the members must have been ten years in the service of the Crown in India, it means that the Indian Civil Service, with its interests and points of view, holds a strong position in the executive. Further, as their promotion to governorships and lieutenant-governorships lies chiefly in the recommendation of the Viceroy, the danger is that they become mere satellites of the Viceroy.

The Governor-General's Executive Council differs from a Cabinet (1) in that the members comprising a Cabinet ordinarily are members of the same political party as the Prime Minister, with a common policy and common political ideals, and (2) in that it can ignore and does ignore adverse votes of the Assembly. In other words, the Governor-General and the Executive Council are "irremovable" and "untouchable" by the chosen representatives of India in the National Assembly.

In ordinary circumstances the Governor-General is bound by the decision of the majority of his Executive Council, and if they are equally divided, he has the casting vote; while in measures affecting the safety and tranquillity or interests of British India he can override his Council. Reduced to practical politics, the Governor-General (Viceroy) is a foreign despot, who may be "benevolent" or otherwise, with only the Secretary of State to check him.

The executive work of the Governor-General in Council, often described as the Government of India, is distributed among the following departments: Finance, Foreign, Home, Legislative, Revenue and Military Supply. Each department except the Foreign Department is assigned to one of the members of the Council, with a permanent secretary at the head. The Foreign Department comes under the immediate superintendence of the Viceroy, who becomes, therefore, his own Foreign Minister.

In addition to these nine departments of the secretariat, there are special departments attached to some one of them, like the Post Office and Telegraph, the Survey, and the Railways, which are centrally administered, while Forests, Agriculture, Education and Indian Medical Service, are administered by the local Governments but supervised by the Government of India.

The Legislature

The Indian Legislature is bicameral, consisting of a Council of State, equivalent to our House of Lords, and a Legislative Assembly in imitation of the House of Commons.

The Council of State, as at present constituted, consists of 34 elected members, 6 nominated non-officials, and 20 officials. The electorate numbers about 20.000 voters. The Governor-General appoints the President of the Council from among its members, and its ordinary term is five years.

The Legislative Assembly comprises 103 elected members and 41 nominated members, of whom 26 are officials. The number of electors is under one million. The President is elected by the Assembly from among its members, and its life is three years.

The members of the Governor-General's Executive Council are not *ex-officio* members of either Chamber, but each of them has to be appointed a member of one or other Chamber, and can vote only in the Chamber of which he is a member. Any member of the Executive Council may speak in either Chamber.

The Governor-General has the power to dissolve or extend the term of either Chamber at his own discretion.

A Bill to become law must be passed by both Chambers. In case of disagreement between the Chambers they meet and vote conjointly. The Governor-General has power to return a Bill for reconsideration by either Chamber.

Women have not the vote and are not eligible for election, but educated public opinion is growing in their favour.

The constituencies are divided into non-Mohammedan, Mohammedan, European, non-European, Sikh and special constituencies of Landholders and Chambers of Commerce. The franchise for general constituencies is based on (1) community, (2) residence, and (3) (*a*) occupation or ownership of a building, (*b*) assessment to, or payment of, municipal or cantonment rates or taxes or local cesses, or (4) the holding of land or membership of a local body.

The powers of the Indian Legislature are very limited, the limitations standing out in bold relief when compared with the "plenary powers" possessed by the Dominion Legislatures.

No measure affecting (*a*) the public debt or revenues of India; or (*b*) the religion, rites or usages of British subjects in India; or (*c*) the discipline or maintenance of the military, naval or air forces; or (*d*) the relations with foreign princes or States; or (*e*) any provincial subject which has been declared by rules to be subject to legislation by the Indian Legislature; or (*f*) any Act of a local legislature; or (*g*) any Act or ordinance made by the Governor-General, can be introduced at any meeting of either Chamber without the previous sanction of the Governor-General. Further, the Secretary of State alone can raise a loan in England, and the Indian Legislature is debarred from passing any law affecting in any way this power of the Secretary of State.

The Annual Estimates of Expenditure are laid before

both Chambers, but no proposals of any revenue or moneys for any purpose can be made except on the recommendation of the Governor-General. Any demand for money or provision for any tax, or the whole Finance Bill, may be refused by the Legislature, but this refusal becomes null and void in view of the power of the Governor-General to restore them by "certification," which he did in the cases of the Finance Bill and the Salt Tax when thrown out by the Assembly. Certain heads of expenditure are "protected" from, and "non-votable" by, the Legislature, for example, Army and Foreign Department, the Church of England in India, the salaries and pensions of the members of the Imperial services. The Governor-General has allowed the Assembly to discuss the Army Budget, but it is not put to the vote. The salaries and pensions in the superior services have been fixed by the Executive Government without the concurrence of the Legislature, and the increases given by the Islington and Lee Commissions were without the consent or the approval of the Assembly. The increases under the Lee Commission were rejected, in fact, by the Legislative Assembly by sixty-eight votes to forty-six, a verdict which was reversed by the Upper Chamber. Pandit Motilal Nehru, the leader of the Swaraj party, in the debate on the recommendations of the Lee Commission, maintained that "the present constitution of the Indian services was an anachronism, and that the Government was attempting the impossible task of working a reformed constitution by means of an unreformed administrative machine."

The conclusion that any fair-minded person is driven to is that the control of the Indian Legislature over Finance and the Civil Service and the Executive amounts to nothing, and that its powers of legislation are limited by the Council of State and the superior powers of the Governor-General and the Secretary of State, whose veto is final. Beyond criticism and the formation of public opinion, for which the Government of India cares little, the Indian Legislature possesses no power to shape the destinies of the millions which it represents.

The power of veto of the Governor-General in respect of legislation hangs like the sword of Damocles over the Legislative Assembly. The power of veto of the Crown, as provided for by the Dominion Acts in Australia, Canada, and South Africa, should be enough.

Provincial Governments

The Presidencies of Bengal, Madras and Bombay and the Provinces of the United Provinces, the Punjab, Bihar and Orissa, the Central Provinces and Assam are each governed by a Governor in Council, and in relation to transferred subjects by the Governor with the Ministers appointed. Delhi, Ajmer-Merwara, Coorg and the North-West Frontier Province and Baluchistan are under Chief Commissioners.

Burma was deliberately excluded from the Reform Act of 1919 because it differed so markedly from India historically, racially, etc. Burma, in fact, was independent until 1886, when it was annexed to British India by force of arms.

This annexation was not only resisted by the people of Burma by warlike means, but was in direct opposition to public opinion in India, which was naturally incensed at British Imperialism robbing Burma of its freedom and adding another slave-nation to the Indian Empire.

By Act of Parliament in 1922 Burma became a Governor's province, with an Executive Council and Ministers in conformity with the Government of India Act, 1919.

The Legislative Council of Burma consists of 104 members, of whom 79 are elected and 25 nominated by the Government. The electorate is estimated at upwards of two millions, and women exercise the vote.

The Governors and the members of the Executive Council are appointed by the Crown. Bengal, Bombay and Madras have four members on the executive, two belonging to the Indian Civil Service and two non-officials; and in the United Provinces, the Punjab, Bihar and Orissa, the Central Provinces and Assam, there are two members on each executive.

Dyarchy

The Provincial Governments are divided into two departments — dyarchy — "transferred" and "reserved." The transferred subjects are Local Government, Education, Industries, Sanitation, Excise (except in Assam), Agriculture, Fisheries and Co-operation, and the reserved subjects include Law and Order, Finance, Forests and Irrigation.

The transferred subjects are administered by Ministers appointed by the Governor from among the elected members of the Provincial Legislature, and the reserved subjects by members of the Executive Council, appointed by the Crown. While the members of the Executive Council act on the principle of collective responsibility, each Minister acts more or less on his own responsibility, the Ministers belonging frequently to different political parties. Another distinction between Ministers and members of the Executive seems very anomalous, for whereas the salaries of the former are subject to the control of the Legislative Council, those of the latter are not.

Provincial Legislatures

The numerical strength of the Provincial Councils varies, Bengal leading with 125 members; Madras and the United Provinces following with 118 each; Bombay, 111; Bihar and Orissa, 98; Punjab, 83; the Central Provinces, 70; and Assam, 53. The statute provides that at least 70 per cent. must be elected and not more than 20 per cent. official members in a Council.

The Governor may summon and address a Council, but is not a member himself; he has the right of nominating a certain number of members. The members of the Executive Council are members of the Provincial Councils.

The qualifications for eligibility for election and for inclusion on the electoral roll are similar to those in the case of the Assembly. In Madras, Bombay and the United Provinces the franchise has been extended to women. As only 3 per cent. of the total population have votes, there is a general demand for extension of the franchise. As in the case with the Assembly, the constituencies are cursed with "communal electorates," instead of being put on a democratic basis. In Madras five nominated seats are reserved for the backward communities.

The normal term of a Legislative Council is three years, the Governor holding the same powers as the Governor-General with regard to dissolution, etc. The first Presidents were appointed by the Governors for five years, but are now elected by the Councils *subject to the approval of the Governors.*

The powers of the Governor are almost as great as those of the Governor-General over the Assembly. In the case of reserved subjects the Governor can override the Council; and in cases of emergency he can authorise expenditure *for the carrying on of any departments,* which practically makes his rule *autocratic.* He exercises power of "certification" of Bills relating to reserved subjects, and of the veto in regard to transferred subjects.

In his Executive Council the Governor has a casting vote in case the Council is equally divided, but as he can override his Council, he holds despotic sway over 20 to 60 millions of people.

Recognising Dyarchy as an illogical, if not an entirely ridiculous, system, the Joint Parliamentary Committee expressed the pious opinion that there should be joint deliberation between the two halves of the Provincial Governments, but Parliament made no such provision in the Act. Consequently dyarchy has met with the failure it courted, succeeding only, as Lord Birkenhead indicated, where it was ignored. Ministers in charge of transferred subjects were directly responsible to the Provincial Legislature, while the officials in charge of the reserved subjects were free from all responsibility to the Legislature. The system permitted two opposing policies on the part of the Government, a sort of facing both ways; invited open and concealed antagonism between Ministers responsible for the transferred subjects and Executive officials in control of the reserved; subjected Ministers to the control of the finance officer, who could mutilate or wreck their schemes by refusing to pay the bill; and led Ministers into the bog of contempt, for they were blamed by the electors for the mistakes and follies of their official colleagues, who had no electoral and no public opinion to consider.

Dyarchy divides a house against itself, and for the British Parliament to wait till 1929 before getting rid of this pernicious system, which it ought not to have enforced on India, would be to confess itself as bankrupt in honesty as it was bankrupt in statesmanship in 1919.

The powers of Provincial Councils are extremely curtailed: (1) by the superior powers of the Governor, as we have just seen; (2) because the following subjects are forbidden both discussion and voting on: (*a*) provincial contributions to the Central Government, (*b*) interest and sinking fund charges on loans, (*c*) expenditure of which the amount is presented by law, (*d*) salaries and pensions of persons appointed by the Crown or by the Secretary of State (members of the Imperial services), and (*e*) salaries of the judges of the High Court of the Province and of the Advocate-General; and (3) by statute, which declares that "the local legislature of any province may not, without the previous sanction of the Governor-General, make or take into consideration any law, (*a*) imposing any new tax unless it is a tax exempted by rules made under this Act, or (*b*) affecting the public debt of India, or the customs duties, or any other tax or duty imposed by the Governor-General, or (*c*) affecting the discipline or maintenance of the naval, military or air forces.

The check on the power of initiation by requiring the previous sanction of the Governor-General is further reinforced by the Reservation of Bills Rules, and encourages friction between the central and local Governments.

Another serious limitation consists in the fact that no member of any Provincial Council can introduce without the previous sanction of the Governor, any measure affecting the public revenues of a province or imposing any charge on these revenues. If a member wants to introduce a Bill limiting the increase in the land revenue or revising land revenue assessments, he must first secure the sanction of the Governor, which may be no easy matter. The injustice of this limitation stands out more clearly when it is realised that the landowners are well represented in the Provincial Councils, while the tenants are not.

Any Bills passed by the Councils have to run the gauntlet of three possible vetoes, that of the Governor, the Governor-General and the Crown.

The Civil Services in India

"Unlike other countries, in which the permanent officials are controlled by Ministers, the administrators of India not merely execute a policy: they also initiate it. For many decades the Indian Civil Service was not only an administration, but it was also a Government." In these ominous words the Government Annual Report for 1924–25 reveals the real nature of the Government of India—a bureaucracy—up till 1919, and the Act of Parliament of that year, which Lord Birkenhead declared to be "a remarkable and extremely bold experiment," did nothing more than expose this Government of alien bureaucrats to the criticism and censure of the elected representatives of the people of India, without power of appointment, dismissal, or even reduction of their salaries. The appointment, pay and dismissal of civil servants rests with the Secretary of State. Members of the services are responsible only to the Governor-General and not to the Legislatures. Three out of six ordinary members of the Governor-General's Executive Council represent the Civil Service, and at least half of the Governor's executive in the Provinces are members of the Service; the permanent secretaries of all departments are members of the Civil Service, and the Civil Service commands a majority of posts in the judiciary.

The Civil Service, in which Englishmen nearly monopolise the higher posts, is to-day the *master* instead of the *servant* of India.

Indian opinion insists on the reversal of this monstrous *régime*, and that the Civil Service shall become the servant of India, appointed by and subject to the reconstituted Government of India, and entirely Indianised.

It will be easy for the reader to be able to understand now the formidable opposition of the Indian Civil Service to Swaraj, for Swaraj means an end to its vast powers and privileges and, so far as Englishmen in the service are concerned, subordination to the position of servants or agents of Indian Ministers, a position which their pride of race resents, and, finally, their eradication from the service.

The Civil Service is fighting for its own hand, forgetful of the rights of Indians, and so far it has fought very successfully. When the secret history of the reforms comes to be written, it will be shown that Mr. Montagu was either outwitted or overruled by the bureaucracy—most probably the latter—and his original intentions whittled down to the satisfaction of the bureaucrats in India and the House of Lords in

England. The adoption of the recommendations of the Lee Commission by the British Parliament was another victory for the Civil Service, but in spite of these victories, regarded by some as pyrrhic, British bureaucracy in India is doomed.

Although I have made a few comments *en passant* on the Constitution, I think it might be helpful to the reader and the general public if I went into more detail, and gave my own impressions of the Legislative Assembly and the Provincial Councils from a personal inspection of these institutions in 1926.

Taking the Legislative Assembly at Delhi first, I was favoured in witnessing the opening ceremony of the new session by the Viceroy (Governor-General), Lord Reading, in viceregal robes, made to look like the King or King-Emperor, with bodyguard to right of him and bodyguard to left of him. This introduction of soldiery seemed incongruous, and defensible only on the plea that—

> " All the world's a stage,
> And all the men and women merely players."

Beholding the personage ascend the steps with a regal air and take his seat in a gilded chair placed on a daïs with a cloth of gold, and then, with a royal wave of the hand and with the voice of command, say, " Pray be seated, gentlemen," I was mightily impressed with the mimicry, and muttered between my teeth, " This is imperial fooling worthy of Gilbert and Sullivan, and better than the plain simplicity and rugged solidity of Edward VII.," whom I had seen opening Parliament in the gilded Chamber. In the area sat the President of the Assembly, in wig and gown, dethroned for the time being, just to remind him and the Assembly, whose honour rested in his hands, that both he and the members were as dust at the feet of India's omnipotent dictator.

Then, when a solemn silence filled the air and the people in the galleries, which were full, had assumed a proper aspect of awe, the great man, the greatest tyrant on earth, read his speech in clear, icy and hectoring tones, as the Kaiser used to do when addressing his submissive soldiers on the parade ground, albeit with this marked difference, that defiance on the part of the Viceroy was answered by defiance on the part of India's loyal sons seated on his left, doughty champions, many of whom had served long terms of imprisonment in the fight for national freedom.

If Lord Birkenhead had been by my side and had witnessed this parody of decency, propriety and good feeling, the worm in him would have turned, and he would have cried aloud, "Hesitate not upon the manner of your going, but go at once, unworthy and unfit to overrule, and let an Indian take your place; he, at least, would not add insult to injury, as you have done; he would respect his fellow-countrymen as patriots working at great sacrifice for the good of Indians, while you represent the lowest and the most immoral system in the world—the exploitation of one nation by another, the exploitation of India by England!"

Exit pompously the Viceroy, after delivering his castigation, without waiting for or permitting a debate on his address, contrary to the custom in the Mother of Parliaments, which always discusses the royal address from the throne.

The next day the members reassembled, with their President reinstated in the chair, where the daïs had been the day before, a chair like unto the Speaker's chair in the House of Commons, simple, solid, and substantial, without gilt or cloth of gold. Right worthily did the President, an Indian, elected by the majority of the Assembly, discharge his duties, reminding me of Mr. Speaker Lowther in his palmy days, when his rulings were tested by a certain liveliness from across the Irish Sea.

The arrangements of the Assembly were similar to those in the House of Commons, the members of the Government occupying the benches on the right of the President, and the Opposition those on the left. A very notable difference, however, struck the eye, namely, the benches forming a complete semicircle in the Assembly, whereas in the House of Commons the benches on the right of the Speaker's chair are entirely separated from those on the left by the floor of the House, so that if a member of one English party wishes to join another party he must cross the floor of the House of Commons, while in the Assembly he can move to the central benches, which are chiefly occupied by Independents.

The proceedings of the Assembly follow closely those of the House of Commons, questions with supplementaries coming first, and then motions, Bills, etc.

After a fortnight's attendance at debates, and careful and prolonged examination of the functions and powers of the All India Legislative Assembly, I was forced to the conclusion that the crowning piece of the anatomy of the Montagu-Chelmsford Constitution was an undoubted dud, without power to displace or replace the Government in which it has no confidence, a Government which does not represent the people ;

without power to appoint or dismiss Ministers; *without power of the purse;* without power to reduce the salary of a single bureaucrat; without power to shift a single nail or screw in the "steel frame"; and without the slightest power over the Governor-General (Viceroy), who, instead of being in the position of a constitutional monarch or of the representative of the Crown, as in Canada and the other self-governing colonies, acting on the advice of the Prime Minister, himself subject to the Assembly, is an autocrat with all the powers of a Tsar, who can defy the Assembly, and has defied the Assembly by certifying the Finance Bill over its head, and by spurning its resolutions.

The last time proceedings of this drastic and arbitrary character took place in England civil war ensued. If such drastic and arbitrary action was exercised by the Governor-General of any self-governing colony in the British Empire, that colony would instantly cut the painter and send the Governor-General back to England by the next boat.

In the Introduction I denounce the Constitution of 1919, which was pitchforked on to India without the sanction of India's leaders, as a colossal hoax. But it is far worse: it is counterfeit; the Assembly is made to resemble the House of Commons without an iota of the power of the Mother of Parliaments. The Tsar of all the Russias behaved more honestly and honourably in yielding more power to the first Duma than the British Government did in creating a make-believe Parliament in Delhi. To constitutionalists all over the world it is a question whether England has not done more harm to parliamentary government by establishing mock parliaments in India than Mussolini by openly smashing parliamentary institutions in

Italy, for mock parliaments only bring parliamentary government into contempt.

Cowards and hypocrites abound among British statesmen in England who defend this deceptive imitation, this illegitimate daughter of the Mother of Parliaments, on the ground that Indians should practise provincial autonomy and provincial self-government before enjoying national autonomy and national self-government. When one turns, therefore, to inspect the Provincial Legislative Councils, one naturally expects to discover that the pledge of responsible government has been redeemed, but inspection discloses, as I found in the Legislative Councils of Madras and the Punjab, whose meetings I attended, that the Provincial Councils are feebler and more futile than the All-India Assembly, and further that they are blasted with dyarchy, from which the Legislative Assembly, fortunately, is free.

Dyarchy was condemned by Sir William Marris, the Governor of the United Provinces, as "a complex, confused system, having no logical basis, rooted in compromise, and defensible only as a transitional expedient." Even Lord Birkenhead confessed: "I myself was always very distrustful of the dyarchical principle. It seemed to me to savour of a kind of pedantic and hide-bound Constitution, to which Anglo-Saxon communities have not generally responded, and which in my anticipation was unlikely to make a successful appeal to a community whose political ideals were, thanks in the main to Macaulay, so largely derived from Anglo-Saxon models."

I challenge the Earl of Birkenhead to declare whether the Tory party, for which he is in a position to speak with authority, or any other political party in Great

Britain, in his opinion, would touch this " pedantic and hide-bound Constitution " with a barge pole.

He knows, and every intelligent citizen outside of a lunatic asylum knows, that not even the Tory party would work it, or try to work it, for a day, much less ten years. Then why does he dishonour himself and his country by upbraiding Indian patriots for refusing to do what Tories would not condescend to do, and for declining to co-operate with alien bureaucrats who outrage Indian public opinion and treat the elected representatives of the people in the legislatures as their inferiors?

" Hath not an Indian eyes, hath not an Indian hands, organs, dimensions, senses, affections, passions, fed with the same food, hurt with the same weapons, subject to the same diseases, healed by the same means, warmed and cooled by the same winter and summer, as a Christian is? If you prick Indians do they not bleed? if you poison them, do they not die? and if you wrong them, shall they not revenge? "

It is this treatment as inferiors and slaves that is gall and wormwood to Indians, treatment which is all the more disgraceful and discreditable after British protestations of " equality " and " partnership."

John Morley once said that bad manners in India were not only an offence, but a crime. I was present at a discussion in the Legislative Assembly with regard to the release of political prisoners under the hateful Bengal Ordinance, and heard the laughter of the English officials at the expense of Indian feeling, which runs high on this injustice to Bengal. Needless to say, I was ashamed of my countrymen, and apologised to some of the Indian leaders afterwards, when they replied that they were accustomed to insolence and callousness on the part of British officials in India, that what hurt them most was the attitude of superiority and of lords of the universe of the British Parliament in forcing upon them a Constitution condemning them to a further period of "inferiority and slavery." "If," they continued, the "British Parliament would descend from the Olympian heights of patronage which is so offensive, and meet us in the plains of equality and brotherhood, we could together frame a Constitution which would be satisfactory and honourable to England and satisfactory and honourable to us, retaining India within the Empire. The present Constitution is dishonouring and demoralising to us, impossible to work, and altogether unworthy of the Mother of Parliaments. Give India a Constitution equal to that of Serbia and Poland, which God knows are more backward in civilisation than India, and all will be well."

Speaking of British officials and fitness to rule, common justice demands that I should place on record my observations on this head after attending debates in the Legislative Assembly and some of the Provincial Legislatures in India. With a natural bias in favour of my countrymen, truth compels me to state that I found a definite inferiority in talent among Britons as compared with Indians, and this inferiority was most marked in the Assembly, which is supposed to be responsible for the good government of the whole of British India. Lord Birkenhead is a great authority on "brains," and it would be well if a high sense of duty impelled him to visit India to see for himself this inferiority of the British bureaucrats. According to English standards of fitness to rule, by which his lordship climbed to the highest position but one in the Government of Great Britain, he would be constrained by a sense of justice to award the first prize to Indians, who far surpass their English rivals in brilliancy, wit, logic, knowledge, breadth of vision, and ideals of statesmanship. Comparisons are odious, but his lordship might nevertheless be tempted to liken British Ministers who hold the highest offices of state to babes in the wood alongside of Indian giants.

Looking at, and listening to, these British bureaucrats dumped on India, Lord Birkenhead, with his analytical mind and lively imagination, would ask himself the question, What station in life would these gentlemen, dressed in a little brief authority, occupy in England or Scotland or Wales? How many of them would rise higher than a civil servant, or a private secretary, or a first-class clerk? What percentage of them would even attain to the position of "city fathers" or "legislators" in England? Bold in speculation and prediction, his lordship would decide that not more than 1 or 2 per cent. would rise higher than a first-class clerk in a Government office.

Reduced to its fundamental basis, India is governed by first-class clerks from England with a few lordlings thrown in as governors, and the 1919 Constitution has only concealed their despotic powers by dressing them in constitutional clothes.

The contempt that Indians have for British rule in their country is, therefore, not to be wondered at. The wonder is that they have stood it so long. The new Constitution, instead of reducing this contempt, has increased it, and, worse still, added to it distrust in British pledges, for the counterfeit Constitution has swept away the last shred of faith in British honesty.

All England shrieked when in the exigencies of a life-and-death struggle Germany trampled upon Belgian liberties, and now in piping times of peace all the world wonders at British hypocrisy riveting tyrannical government on India under the pretence of taking Indians into partnership.

Can no good thing come out of evil ? Has nothing good come out of the deformed Councils ? Without answering the metaphysical question we may profitably answer the practical one. Yes ! one great truth, which must have important bearings on the future of India, stands out like a beacon-light on a surf-driven shore, namely, that Indians, judged by English as well as natural standards, are infinitely better fitted to govern India than their English overlords. In sheer intellectual and parliamentary capacity Indians outshine their British adversaries. It is not so much Indians who require lessons in the art of responsible parliamentary government—for they are to the manner born—but Englishmen in India who are like fish out of water.

CHAPTER IV

HOW THE PEOPLE LIVE—THE POVERTY OF THE PEOPLE

ESTIMATES of the average annual income per head of the population :—

Year.	By whom made.	Rupees.	£ s. d. (at the then rate of exchange).
1870	Dadabhai Naoroji . .	20	2 0 0
1882	Sir David Barbour . .	27	2 10 0
1901	Lord Curzon . . .	30	2 0 0
1911	Hon. E. M. Cook . .	50	3 5 0

In 1921 the Statistical Branch of the Madras Department of Agriculture calculated the average annual income of the population of the Presidency at 100 rupees, or about £10, but the rise in prices brought this sum down to the equivalent of 42 rupees in 1899, or a little over £4.

Dr. Harold Mann investigated recently the average income in two Deccan villages. In one it worked out at 44 rupees per head, 25 persons having 77 rupees per head, 137 persons 62 rupees per head, and the remaining 352 only 32 rupees per head, which is insufficient for food and clothing, without payment of interest on debt and other compulsory calls. This means that the majority of the villagers were insolvent and half starved. In the other the average family income amounted to 168·8 rupees, and the cost of living to 219·6 rupees, so that the income only covered two-thirds of the bare cost of living. "Eighty-five per cent. of the families were insolvent, their incomes being only equal to 51·5 per cent. of the sum required for decent subsistence on the most modest scale."

This comparison, showing the diminishing income of the Indian people, startled the big wigs in the British oligarchy, and Lord George Hamilton, Secretary of State for India, referred to it in the House of Commons on August 16th, 1901: "I admit it at once that if it could be shown that India has retrograded in national prosperity under our rule we stand self-condemned, and we ought no longer to be trusted with the control of that country"; while Lord Curzon on March 18th, 1901, upon the debate on the Indian Budget in the Viceregal Council at Calcutta, tried to upset his own estimate of £2 per head per annum by stating: "I do not say that these data are incontrovertible. There is an element of conjecture in these, but so there was in the figures of 1880. . . ."

All that we desire here is to quicken the conscience of the British people (1) by presenting a true picture of poverty and unemployment in India, and (2) by discussing their chief causes with a view to their amelioration or removal as far as possible.

Since 1901 there has been no official estimate of the income of the people—an unreasonable negligence on the part of the Government, which produces a Statistical Abstract every year at some cost to the Indian taxpayer. The Statistical Abstract does, however, supply data from which the terrible poverty may be deduced.

Let us consider the figures for the relief of famine, which is both a consequence and a cause of poverty. Apart from charitable organisations like the Indian Famine Fund of the Lord Mayor of London, the Government of India disburses every year in and year out financial aid in relief of "the extreme, the abject, the awful, poverty of the Indian people."

From the Statistical Abstract furnished by the Government of India :—

Famine Relief

	£		Rupees.
1900–01	4,147,177	1911–12	17,14,403
1901–02	884,061	1912–13	28,33,278
1902–03	983,090	1913–14	23,62,671
1903–04	905,680	1914–15	41,98,277
1904–05	1,000,009	1915–16	11,20,420
1905–06	1,000,930	1916–17	28,14,254
1906–07	1,009,743	1917–18	56,476
1907–08	1,296,063	1918–19	46,16,514
1908–09	1,645,179	1919–20	1,17,46,559
1909–10	1,000,000	1920–21	26,64,017
	£13,871,902		Rs. 3,40,27,069

For the first decade of the twentieth century the Government therefore spent on an average more than a million pounds sterling annually to help the famine-stricken, and in the second decade more than 340 crores of rupees.

With regard to the number of famines and loss of life, Mr. Digby supplied the following from official records :—

Famines

Periods.	Numbers.	Deaths (Estimated or Recorded).
1800 to 1825 .	5	1,000,000
1826 to 1850 .	2	500,000
1851 to 1875 .	6	5,000,000
1876 to 1900 .	18	26,000,000

For 1901 to 1925 the world awaits official figures.

The *Lancet* estimated the death-roll from actual starvation or the diseases arising therefrom for 1890 to 1900 at 19,000,000. Sir Antony MacDonald, President of a Famine Commission, spoke of how the people "died like flies." Mr. Digby compared the loss of life by famine in India during the ten years 1891–1900 at 19,000,000 with the loss of life by war in all the world during one hundred and seven years (1793–1900) at 5,000,000.

The chief lesson which these figures of famine and famine relief teach us is that famine has come to stay in India, that famine is chronic, that in spite of efforts of the Government of India this scourge of humanity still tortures the poor of India.

For an exhaustive examination of famine the reader must consult the volumes written on the subject both by English and Indians and the reports of the many Famine Commissions. By way of question and answer I shall endeavour to bring out some of its salient features.

As we live in an age of materialism, which is careless of human values and counts famine as a good purge sent by God to correct the reproductive capacities of

Indians, who do not practise Malthusian restriction of the race as their Christian overlords do, the question of the financial loss incurred by famine comes first, and is partly answered by the above figures for famine relief and by Mr. Digby, who estimated that two big famines in the last decade of the nineteenth century involved a loss of £120,000,000 each. Hence a vicious circle set up of poverty causing famine and famine causing poverty. Severe famine might be described as due to rain failure and poor monsoons falling upon impoverished people.

What evidence suggests that the Government of India regards famine as chronic? The establishment of the Famine Code in 1880, which provides palliatives on a permanent basis for the relief of famine. This is one of the wisest and most humane achievements of the bureaucracy, of which we can all be proud.

To the question whether Indian famines are more destructive to health and life than in ancient days Mr. Digby gives an answer in the affirmative, asserting that aforetime famine only arose after two years of drought, whereas now one year's failure of rain at the right time for agricultural operations leads to acute famine. Then grain stores in the villages mitigated the suffering; now, since the development of the railways, the surplus stores are exported, and prices rise with this artificial scarcity, so that millions have not the wherewithal to buy food. This point is emphasised by Mr. Vaughan Nash in his book on "The Great Famine," namely, that even in famine years food enough is grown in India for all, but at a price beyond the purchasing power of the people. Hence "fever" has a massacre of innocents every year according to the Statistical Abstract, "fever," which an Anglo-

Indian medical authority defined as "a euphemism for insufficient food, scanty clothing and unfit dwellings."

What is the remedy for famine? In 1878 Sir Arthur Cotton advocated "irrigation" as a great remedy, and the Famine Commissioners, in their report in 1880, said:—

"Among the means that may be adopted for giving India *direct protection from famine arising from drought, the first place must unquestionably be assigned to works of irrigation.* It has been too much the custom, in discussions as to the policy of constructing such works, to measure their value by their financial success, considered only with reference to the net return to Government on the capital invested in them. The true value of irrigation works is to be judged very differently. First must be reckoned the direct protection afforded by them in years of drought by the saving of human life, by the avoidance of loss of revenue remitted and of the outlay incurred in costly measures of relief. But it is not only in years of drought that they are of value. In seasons of average rainfall they are of great service and a great source of wealth, giving certainty to all agricultural operations, increasing the out-turn per acre of the crops, and enabling more valuable descriptions of crops to be grown. From the Punjab in the north to Tinnevelly, at the southern extremity of the peninsula, wherever irrigation is practised, such results are manifest; and we may see rice, sugar-cane, or wheat taking the place of millets or barley, and broad stretches of indigo growing at a season when unwatered lands must lie absolutely unproductive."

How has the Government of India acted upon the advice of its greatest engineer and of its own commission? From 1882 to 1898 it spent, according to Mr. Digby, from revenue nearly seven times more on railways than on irrigation works, and from capital more than six times as much; and from 1898 to 1926 its policy has been one of comparative starvation of irrigation, India's chief means of redemption. When the increased productivity of the soil—probably four-fold—and the cheaper communication by navigable canals from irrigation are taken into account, the policy of the Government becomes incomprehensible, except on the theory that Imperialism got hold of the Government, and that strategic railways found greater favour in its sight. How many famines, how much loss of life and money, how much impoverishment, might have been avoided if the Government had pursued a bolder policy of irrigation, history will relate.

The Government missed its opportunities, and, in the words of Mr. Digby, "discredit has taken the place of what would have been a monument of unassailable praise."

Coming to the economic conditions of present times, I cannot do better than recommend the reader to study the recent publications (1925) of Mr. Pillai—"Economic Conditions in India"—and of Mr. Darling—"The Punjab Peasant in Prosperity and Debt"—in each of which he will find a gold mine of information and suggestion.

In the introductory note to Mr. Pillai's work, Professor Gilbert Slater writes: "The poverty of India is a grim fact. In the main it is, as Mr. Pillai shows, the result, not of unequal distribution of what wealth is produced, excessively large incomes being very few, though conspicuous, as of a very small production *per capita*. A reasonable estimate of money income would be, for the present day, somewhere about 100 rupees per annum, or 4½d. per day. Taking the whole population together, rich and poor, it may be said that about two-fifths of the available income must be spent merely on the grains that form the basis of the Indian dietary—rice, millets, and wheat—leaving only 3*d*. per head per day for all other foods, including even such indispensable supplements as salt and pulse, for clothing, education, medical aid, housing, religious festivals and observances, all the luxurious expenditure of the relatively inconsiderable number of well-to-do families, and the conventional necessities of rare indulgences of the poor, such as tobacco, betel, toddy, and a modicum of jewellery. This, or something like this, being the average condition, that of the poorest classes can be guessed. A detailed examination, family by family, of a Madras Parchery, *i.e.*, a pariah settlement, in the middle of the city, by Mr. Ramachandran, Reader in Economics to the University, showed an average income of only 2¼d. per head per day, which means only ½d. per day in addition to a bare sufficiency of rice; and a very recent inquiry by Mr. Ranga Nayakulu yielded an estimate of 30 rupees—45*s*.—per annum as the average income per head for the labourers of untouchable castes in the Godavari delta."

This estimate of 4½d. per day compares favourably with Lord Curzon's estimate of less than 2*d*. in 1901, but unfortunately there must be set against it higher prices, the retail prices of food grains rising from 100 in 1873 to 114 in 1894, 117 in 1905, 168 in 1910, and to 222 in 1914.

Professor Slater goes on to say: "This estimate of 30 rupees per annum may be unduly pessimistic, but of these people and of the kindred castes of Pallans,

Parayans, Cherumas, etc., on whose toil the cultivation of the rice fields of Southern India mainly depends, it may be said generally that their earnings in grain and coin barely suffice for the subsistence of families large enough to maintain their members from one generation to another, the surplus offspring dying, that they are habitually hungry, and that it is only because they make their own huts in their spare time, collect their own fuel, need scarcely any clothing, and enjoy abundant sunshine that they can subsist at all."

To go back to the nineteenth century, Sir C. A. Elliott, K.C.S.I., Lieutenant-Governor of Bengal, said when he was Settlement Officer of the North-Western Province: "I do not hesitate to say that half our agricultural population never know from year's end to year's end what it is to have their hunger fully satisfied," and "half our agricultural population means 100 MILLIONS OF PEOPLE"; and Sir William Hunter, discoursing on "England's Work in India," and discussing normal, not abnormal, conditions, said in 1880, "There remain 40 millions of people who go through life on insufficient food."

Returning to present times, Mr. Darling, after making an exhaustive study of the peasant proprietors of the Punjab, wrote: "The first and most obvious conclusion is that the bulk of the cultivators of the Punjab 'are born in debt, live in debt, and die in debt.' Probably in no district are more than a third free from debt, and in some the percentage is less than ten." And, again, the same trustworthy investigator concluded: "So far as the rest of India and its 300 millions are concerned, no one can doubt that the supreme need of the country is food, more food, and still more food."

Referring to the economic conditions in the towns—and it is well to note that the census figures show that of the total population 10·1 per cent. live in towns and 89·9 per cent. in the villages—Professor Slater observes that "the Bombay investigations quoted by Mr. Pillai show an average income per head for a large number of working-class families of 149 rupees—£11 3*s*. 6*d*. That this should be considerably more than the average income measured in money for the whole Indian population is a significant fact; it shows, on the one hand, to how small an extent the average income of all India is swollen by the incomes of the few rich, and, on the other, the effect of the extra cost of city life in forcing up wages, for, in spite of his relatively high money income, the condition of the Bombay cotton operative or dock labourer is deplorable, far worse than that of the average villager, and scarcely better than that of the untouchable village coolie."

Cotton Wages in the Mills in May, 1921
(Average earnings per day)

Centre.	Men.	Women.	Big Lads and Children.	All Work-people.
	*Rs. p. a.	Rs. p. a.	Rs. p. a.	Rs. p. a.
Bombay .	1 5 6	0 10 9	0 11 1	1 2 10
Ahmedabad .	1 5 0	0 12 1	0 11 4	1 2 7
Sholapur .	0 15 11	0 6 9	0 9 1	0 12 8
Other centres .	1 1 8	0 10 1	0 8 11	0 15 6

* 1 rupee = 1*s*. 6*d*.; 16 annas = 1 rupee; 1 anna = 12 pies.

From the table of Mr. Findlay Shirras (Report on the Wages and Hours Inquiry in the Bombay Cotton

Mills) one learns at a glance the sweated wages of the cotton industry.

This averages out at less than 2*s*. a day of eleven hours for men, 1*s*. per day for women, and from 4*d*. to 6*d*. for children working half-time. Fines for being late, for absence, or for inferior work still further reduce these low wages, and the common practice of deferring payment for a month lands the poor worker in the ditch of debt, out of which many never climb, having to scale heights of interest varying from 75 to 300 per cent.

Well may the people suffer from lack of food, and the country from under-production because of under-consumption! Well may the people die like flies from disease because of sub-normal vitality! Well may the Government find favour in the eyes of capitalists when it makes it easy for them to bleed the workers white, and to keep them in a chronic state of moral and physical lassitude, so that both the will to strike and the capacity to strike successfully for better conditions are reduced to vanishing point!

The monetary and materialistic interests—the basest interests of mankind—of the British bureaucracy and of capitalism unite them in a common policy of political and economic subjection of the people of India.

The number of people employed in the cotton industry approximated in 1923 to 347,380, of whom 66,226 were women and 15,766 children, working nearly 8 million spindles and 145,000 looms.

In 1921 the relative position between Great Britain and India was—

	India.		United Kingdom.
Looms . .	123,783	...	790,399
Spindles . .	6,870,804	...	60,053,246

All told, there are 280 cotton mills in India, producing annually about 700,000,000 lb. of yarn and 400,000,000 lb. of woven goods. Exports of cotton manufactures, chiefly to China, Egypt, Persia, Asiatic Turkey, Arabia, East Africa, and the Straits Settlements, averaged annually in rupees—

1909 to 1914.	1914 to 1919.	1920.	1921.
20,895,000 ..	43,043,000 ..	87,362,000 ..	75,063,000

The paid-up capital in the mills in 1920 was estimated at £258,888, or 271,000,000 rupees, the debenture capital amounting to £99,000, or 34,229,472 rupees. According to the estimate of the Chairman of the Mill-owners' Association, the gross profits of the Bombay mills in 1920–21 amounted to 16 crores of rupees, or £16,000,000 sterling, the dividends of thirty-five leading mills averaging 59 per cent.

As representative men have said in the House of Commons that England holds India for Lancashire, reference may briefly be made to the competition in cotton. In his reply to the Lancashire cotton trade deputation in 1917, Mr. Austen Chamberlain said that "the proportion of your Lancashire trade with which Indian mills are in effective competition does not amount to more than 2 per cent. of your whole trade"; and His Majesty's Senior Trade Commissioner in India computed the competition in bleached goods at below 5 per cent. in 1919.

Mr. Pillai observes that "the imposition of the excise duty of 3·5 per cent. to countervail the import duty has all along been felt as a grievous national insult and a standing monument to Lancashire's domination over India's industrial life." Thanks to the strike in 1925 of the sweated mill operatives of

Bombay against a reduction in wages, the Government of India came to the rescue of the mill-owners, suspending the excise duty, which no future Government is ever likely to reimpose.

On the question of competition it is necessary to note that imports of Japanese cotton goods have risen from 2·6 million yards in 1913 to 207 million yards in 1918, and that the Indian export of yarn to China is less than half what it was ten years ago, due to displacement by Japanese yarn. The chief factor in explanation of these changes seems to be the cheapness of Japanese labour, because in Japan three women-workers are employed to every male worker, while in India women number less than one-fifth of the workers, and the wages of women in Japan are about three-fourths of men's.

This is one more illustration of Capital all the world over exploiting Labour, and emphasises the need for the workers of the world to unite.

The Jute Industry

The jute industry exhibits the best example of the two extremes of riches and poverty and of the merciless exploitation of Labour by Capital. The figures in the table on p. 98 indicate the profits of Indian jute mills. Adding the reserve accumulations to the profits, this works out at 90 per cent. per annum. Not bad for capital provided half by Britons and half by Indians! Labour's share in this plunder may be estimated from the weekly wages paid to the workers, amounting to 3*s*. for carders, 3*s*. 6*d*. for rowers, 4*s*. 9*d*. for spinners, 7*s*. for hemmers and sewers, 9*s*. for weavers, and 12*s*. for tenters. Out of these princely earnings weavers have to pay to the foreman about 13*s*. for " footing " and from 1*d*. to 2*d*. a week as " backsheesh."

Year.	Profits before paying Debenture Interest.
	Rupees.
1913 . .	24,597,553
1914 . .	9,618,694
1915 . .	42,148,960
1916 . .	64,871,041
1917 . .	42,392,573
1918 . .	122,925,767
1919 . .	116,453,696
1920 . .	125,382,066
1921 . .	49,586,331
1922 . .	35,835,863
1923 . .	49,533,808

Under this system of blackmail and meagre wages the lot of the labourer is not a happy one, for he is driven into the hands of the money-lender, who hesitates at nothing in the way of interest. As the management of the mills is almost entirely English, this state of affairs reflects badly on our industrial morality.

This industry, which flourishes chiefly in Bengal, has had a rapid rise in production from 8 tons a day in 1855 to 4,000 tons a day in 1924, and now does two-thirds of the trade which Dundee used to do in its pristine days, when it supplied half the world's output. Scotsmen transferred their affections from the Tay to the Hooghly, where labour was cheap, and the raw material near, and the prospects of profit big. The accuracy of their prehensile instincts has been proved by the bloated dividends and reserve funds in excess of the capital of the Indian mills, which to-day consume five times as much jute as the Dundee mills.

India, as Mr. Brailsford prettily put it, is the jewel in the British crown for capitalists, but for the dumb-driven Indian labourers it is still a treadmill.

Plantations

Wages on the tea, rubber, coffee, cotton, oil, pepper, etc., plantations average 3*s.* to 4*s.* a man, 1*s.* 6*d.* to 3*s.* for a woman. On the tea plantations of Assam a man gets 8*d.* for eight hours a day, a woman 6*d.*, and a child 3*d.*; in the tea factories the worker earns 9*d.* for an eight-hour working day.

The coolie suffers not only from this low level of wages, but frequently from indebtedness to his employers in outlandish districts, where he is dependent upon the shops provided by the employers for his foodstuffs, fuel, etc. This indebtedness, together with the isolation of the plantation, renders it difficult for him to seek employment elsewhere, and thus practically reduces him to a life of economic slavery. His treatment often borders on the inhuman, and his chances of justice and redress of grievances are chimerical.

The author of "Uncle Tom's Cabin" would find in too many plantations facts upon which to write another story to stir the indignation of the world.

As a great deal of British capital is sunk in these undertakings, with the tainted profits coming directly into British pockets, and as the British people are the boastful trustees of India, it is time that the British Parliament ended this state of slave labour or put up its shutters. It is no good leaving these disgraceful and disreputable labour conditions in the factories, mines and plantations of India in the hands of the

Government of India, under whose ægis they have grown and flourished.

Of course the right remedy is government by Indians for Indians.

The Coal Industry

I had the pleasure of inspecting some of the coal mines and mining villages at Jharia (Bihar) in the company of Sir Bupendranath Mitra, the Minister of Labour, one of the few Indians whom the British bureaucracy has allowed to rise to a high position in the Civil Service of his country, and of Mr. Joshi, M.L.A., and Mr. Chaman Lal, M.L.A., the redoubtable leaders of Labour.

My impressions of the economic, scientific, sanitary, housing—in spite of the boards of health which have recently been established—and moral conditions which I saw were anything but favourable. The capitalist who ran the mines, whether Englishman or Indian—most of the mines are in the hands of British capitalists, which means that the profits go to England—evidently did not belong to the same school as the American capitalist, who believes in high wages as concomitant with high efficiency, as the following figures taken from the report of the Chief Inspector of Mines will show :—

	Hours.	Weekly Wages.
Miners	40	R's. 4·12 = 7*s.*
Underground males (other than miners)	52	,, 3·12 = 5*s.*
Underground females	48	,, 2·8 = 3*s.* 9*d.*
Surface males	60	,, 3·15 = 5*s.* 11*d.*
Surface females	60	,, 2·7 = 3*s.* 8*d.*

In 1922 disputes often recurred over demands for higher wages. The number of persons working in the mines regulated by the Indian Mines Act was 229,511, of whom 142,103 were men, 78,806 women, and 8,602 children under twelve. Prohibition of employment of children underground under thirteen years of age came into force in 1924, but 60,000 women still go down into the bowels of the earth to struggle in dust and dirt and damp for a bare existence.

In one of the mines we inspected, where the coal was near the surface, strings of coolie women were employed in carrying the coal in baskets on their heads up steep inclines, a sight which made us pause when we thought of the much-advertised blessings which Western civilisation had brought to India.

From the human and economic point of view the most distressing feature of the mines was this large amount of female labour employed underground, in conditions inimical to the health and morals of the women, involving unnecessary risks to their progeny, and dangerous to the standard of wages of the men. When challenged, the representatives of the mine-owners defended this evil system on the flimsy and questionable ground that the miners liked to have their womenfolk working with them in order to augment their earnings. To soothe our offended susceptibilities, we were assured by the English management that from 60 to 80 per cent. of the women were actually wives of the miners.

A candid capitalist would confess that Great Britain holds India for cheap labour and big profits.

The lessons which one learnt from this inspection of one of the most important coalfields of India were—(1) the utter unworthiness of British rulers to act as trustees for the working classes of India; (2) the need of trade boards to regulate wages; and (3) the imperative need of powerful trade unions, which at present are in their infancy, in order to protect Labour from the gargantuan greed of Capitalism. Some whole-hoggers would go much further and urge the elimination of Capitalism by Nationalisation of the mines, but personally I should prefer complete self-government for India as a natural and proper precedent in the evolution of India's economic freedom.

The Labour party in Great Britain may think that it has got a difficult enough task to hoe its own row at home without travelling far East; nevertheless I urge upon its serious consideration, firstly, that in the fight against Capitalism the economic conditions of the East may determine the economic conditions of the West, and, secondly, that the British Labour party is morally involved in responsibility for the disgraceful exploitation of labour in India as long as Great Britain rules over that country. In short, the British Labour party cannot shirk, either in its own selfish interests or in the interests of its downtrodden fellow-workers, its share of responsibility for the grinding poverty of India.

Economics of Agricultural Villages

Mr. Jack, Settlement Officer, estimated the agricultural incomes in Faridpur, Bengal, at an average of 50 rupees per head, 49·5 per cent. of the agricultural families living in *comfort* on an annual joint income of 365 rupees, 28·5 per cent. living *below comfort* on 233 rupees, 18 per cent. *above want* on 166 rupees, and 4 per cent. in indigence on 115 rupees.

Dr. Lucas's researches into village life in the Punjab led him to the conclusion that "from 20 to 30 per cent.

of all the villages were equally poverty-stricken," as the village of Kabirpur, where the gross income of an agricultural family, consisting of 4·5 members, worked out at 85 rupees 10 annas 8 pies plus 22·58 maunds of wheat and maize.

As an index to the economic conditions of a people, the expenditure on the necessaries and luxuries of life is an alternative to the average income per head. According to Dr. Engel, the lower the percentage expenditure on physical necessities the higher is the economic prosperity. The following analyses speak for themselves:—

Items.	Day-labourer.	Agriculturist.	Black-smith.	Shop-keeper.	Poor Middle Class.
	Per cent.	Per cent.	Per cent.	Per cent.	Per cent.
Food . . .	95·4	94·0	79·0	77·7	74·0
Clothing . .	4·0	3·0	11·0	9·0	4·7
Medicine . . .	—	1·0	5·0	5·9	8·0
Education . .	—	—	—	1·0	3·3
Religious and social ceremonies . .	0·6	2·0	4·0	5·0	8·0
Luxuries . . .	—	—	1·0	1·4	2·0
Total . .	100	100	100	100	100

(From Professor Radhakamal Mukerji's "Foundations of Indian Economics.")

Class.	Food.	Clothing.	Other Necessaries.	Sundries.	Total Income.	Total Expenses.	Members in Family.
	£ s. d.	£ s. d.	£ s. d.	£ s. d.	£ s. d.	£ s. d.	
1. Petty clerk	26 0 0	4 0 0	4 0 0	4 10 0	40 0 0	38 10 0	
2. Domestic servant .	7 15 0	?	0 10 0	4 10 0	17 0 0	12 15 0	2·5
3. Agricultural labourer .	4 15 0	0 15 0	0 10 0	—	6 0 0	6 0 0	4·5

(From Professor Horne's examination of a Patna village.)

My own observations of the economic conditions in the villages I give with diffidence for what they are worth. One village within twenty miles of Madras, chosen at random, consisted of about seventy houses, with a population approaching 500. Two brothers, with their wives and four children each, owned and cultivated about 4 acres of land, from which they raised two crops of "paddy" and one crop of "ragi" every year, the average annual income amounting to 180 rupees—270*s.* From this they paid 30 rupees per annum to the Government for land revenue, and 2 rupees for road tax. They had two pairs of oxen for ploughing, which cost about 60 rupees a year to keep fit, and which were used for other operations during eight months of the year, bringing in about 60 rupees. Off and on both brothers and their families went out to work on other lands for hire during five or six months a year, the men earning 4 to 6 annas (6*d.* to 9*d.*) a day for ten hours, and the women and boys 2 annas (3*d.*) per day, with one meal per day thrown in. This was the average scale of wages in the district. Sometimes they found precarious labour in Madras city, driving carts, etc. They lived on the joint family system, occupying one house, made half of clay and half of brick, with a courtyard and two or three tiny rooms off. Furniture was conspicuous by its absence. The men and boys wore a cloth round the loins, and the women a sari, which folded over the body. They partook of one meal a day at home, which consisted of rice, and another meal of gruel provided by the employer when working on hire. They were in debt to the money-lender, paying 15 per cent. compound interest, because he was more lenient in regard to repayments than the co-operative society, which only charged 9 per cent.

interest, but demanded punctual payments. They found it hard to keep body and soul together, and in case of sickness it became impossible to make ends meet, when they were compelled to have recourse to the money-lender again, and fell deeper into debt and poverty.

I cite the case of these brothers because it is typical of the cultivators. The landless labourers, who number eighty in the village, suffer from *chronic starvation* because of irregularity of employment and low wages.

Some peasant proprietors had been reduced to landless labourers, having been compelled to sell their holdings in order to liquidate their debts to the money-lender.

There is no poor law system to relieve their chilling poverty and to assuage their dire distress, the poor depending upon the charity of the poor. I might add that there was no Government school in this village, although the villagers desired free and compulsory education. The Christian missionary school did not command the confidence of the parents. The village was without any provision for medical aid, the nearest dispensary being seven miles distant. A "toddy" shop, licensed by the Government, did not add to the material or moral welfare of the poor villagers.

When I asked the villagers with their headman if they had any grievances against the Government, they complained that wild boars from the neighbouring forest damaged their crops, and the Government refused to pay them any compensation. They desired Government permission to clear the forest and cultivate the soil, but, I presume, the forest was reserved for Englishmen to indulge in the refined sport of "pigsticking " at the expense of the village. They evinced political consciousness, for they wanted Swaraj both locally and nationally. Locally a panchyate (village council) would act as a check upon the village officer of the Government, who, in his capacity of collector of revenue and judge, had a monopoly of power, and often acted tyrannically, even to the extent of exacting labour without payment. Mahatma Gandhi was their national hero, to whom they looked for deliverance from their British persecutors.

In other villages which I visited in Bihar, Punjab, etc., I found the economic conditions very similar to those in the Madras Presidency. Everywhere the struggle for existence was terrible, unemployment during many months of the year constant, starvation common, especially amongst the expropriated, dispossessed, and landless classes, wages low, hours of labour long, taxation of land high, preventable disease prevalent, housing bad and overcrowded, sanitation, education, and medical aid most defective or absent altogether.

In a village near Delhi my heart was gladdened to meet with one student, the only claimant to education in the village, for there was no school, who, like my countrymen in Scotland, had a rare yearning for learning, and who by superhuman efforts overcame his surroundings of poverty and attended the University of Delhi.

To what depths of poverty and semi-starvation the people had sunk in another village may be gleaned from the fact that petty thieving by night had become a recognised institution.

In every village I asked if there were any cases of starvation, when the replies varied from " Half the village goes to sleep hungry every night" to "Many never eat one square meal a day."

Lean faces and ill-nourished bodies of men, women and children formed circumstantial evidence of underfeeding which no doctor could neglect.

Humiliated and distressed beyond measure by what I had seen in the villages and coalfields of India, betokening poverty and misery beyond the dreams of poverty, my greatest humiliation and distress was experienced in Orissa, a district afflicted by chronic famine and starvation, where a deputation of men, naked except as to their loins, waited upon me to invoke my aid on behalf of its starving people. Accustomed to horrid shapes and sights unholy which I saw as a doctor before the war in mangled men from accidents while the Forth Bridge was being built, during the Great War in the frightfully wounded, fresh from the field of battle, and in the general carnage and death on a torpedoed ship, and since the war in a railway smash close to Lyons, when I rendered first aid to my fellow-passengers, including fair women, young and old, as well as men with faces mutilated, throats cut, and feet hanging by sinews to lacerated stumps, my feelings of horror and anguish were more deeply moved by the sight of these victims of famine and starvation, these walking skeletons, these bags of bones, in suspended animation, these emaciated human wrecks, with sunken eyes, from which all fire and hope had departed, than by the sight of the victims of man's inhumanity to man, or of the victims of engineering enterprise. Perhaps my greatest horror and anguish arose from the facts, firstly, that I, as a British citizen, was responsible for their physical condition, leading to a slow and painful death, inasmuch as I was responsible for the Government which failed to prevent famine by greater schemes of irrigation and by reducing the assessment of land, and failed to provide sufficient food for the starving populations, and, secondly, because of my inability to render them any direct succour.

I shall conclude this chapter on the poverty of India by three quotations. First, from the Indian Constitutional Reforms Report of 1918: "The Indian Government compiles no statistics showing the distribution of wealth, but such incomplete figures as we have obtained show that the number of persons enjoying a substantial income is very small. In one province the total number of persons who enjoyed an income of £66 a year derived from other sources than land was 30,000; in another province, 20,000. The revenue and rent returns also show how small the average agricultural holding is. According to one estimate, the number of landlords whose income derived from their proprietary holdings exceeds £20 a year in the United Provinces is about 126,000 out of a population of 48 millions. It is evident that the curve of wealth descends very steeply, and that enormous masses of the population have little to spare for more than the necessaries of life." Secondly, in 1918–19 the number paying income tax, which was assessed only on non-agricultural incomes of 1,000 rupees and upwards per annum, in British India aggregated only 366,431; and thirdly, the Material and Moral Progress Report for 1922 tells us that the masses of the Indian population "are beset with poverty of a kind which finds no parallel in the more exigent, because less tropical, countries of Europe."

CHAPTER V

REMEDIES FOR POVERTY

HAVING indicated generally the nature and extent of poverty in India, we wish now to summarise the remedies. In India, one-fifth of the human race lies crushed between the upper and lower millstones of Capitalism and Imperialism, suffering tortures of body, mind and spirit that only the pen of Milton could adequately portray. The sport and playground of these two evil and inhuman forces for centuries, India is peculiarly fitted for the great solvents of Socialism and Self-government. As the history of the world teaches that political emancipation precedes economic emancipation, self-government should come first.

The working classes of Great Britain, Germany and France emerged out of the darkness and despair of economic slavery more by means of the vote than by barricades and industrial strife, and it is reasonable to infer that their comrades in India will have to travel along the same road in their fight for freedom. In this respect one is glad to note that the Swaraj party favours adult suffrage, which British Imperialists fear.

Self-government, therefore, holds the first place in my judgment as a remedy for Indian poverty, for it is idle and vain to expect British rulers to act otherwise than they have done since the battle of Plassey, to act otherwise than in the interests of British Capitalism. Sir John Strachey confessed the truth when he said :

"We are often told that it is the duty of the Government of India to think of Indian interests alone, and that if the interests of Manchester suffer it is no affair of ours. For my part, I utterly repudiate such doctrines. I have not ceased to be an Englishman because I have passed the greater part of my life in India, and have become a member of the Indian Government. The interests of Manchester, at which foolish people sneer, are the interests not only of the great and intelligent population engaged directly in the trade of cotton, but of millions of Englishmen. I am not ashamed to say that . . . there is no higher duty in my estimation than that which I owe to my own country." Hence the policy of the Government of India has been to consider the interests of England before those of India, to encourage the export of raw material from India for the benefit of Lancashire, and to discourage manufactures which would compete with English manufactures, first by tariffs penalising the import of Indian manufactured goods into England and secondly, after the adoption of Free Trade by England, by handicapping Indian enterprise by the levy of the countervailing excise duty on cotton goods.

Referring to the cotton duties, Mr. Lovat Fraser reported that they have done more to impair the moral basis upon which British rule is supposed to rest than any other act of the British in India.

By way of contrast in ideals and ethics to those of Sir John Strachey compare the attitude of Sir Alexander Galt, Minister of Finance for Canada, when the Colonial Office and the British Chambers of Commerce protested against the right of Canada to erect her own tariff system. "Self-government," he wrote in a memorable despatch, "would be utterly annihilated if the views of the Imperial Government were to be preferred to those of the people of Canada. It is, therefore, the duty of the present Government distinctly to affirm the right of the Canadian Legislature to adjust the taxation of the people in the way they deem best, even if it should happen to meet with the disapproval of the Imperial Ministry."

The Imperial spirit boasted by Sir John Strachey—the spirit of exploitation of the conquered by the conqueror, of the weak by the strong, of Labour by Capitalism, of the Indian by the Englishman—is the spirit in which India has been governed both under the East India Company and under the British crown.

The Directors of the East India Company made no secret about their aims and objects in India; they made no hypocritical professions of philanthropy, of ruling India for the good of Indians, or of teaching Indians to rule themselves; the measure of the success of their agents and administrators was not the contentment and happiness, the moral and material progress, of the people; the Ten Commandments found no place in the rules and regulations issued for the guidance of their servants in dealing with Indians; their first and last object in India was business, big business, profits, more profits, to get rich quickly, honestly if possible, but if not, to get rich quickly. Inspired by these motives of pelf and plunder, Indian industries waned while British industries waxed; Indians became poorer while Englishmen grew richer; India impoverished, England enriched.

In the early days of the East India Company "the business of a servant of the Company was simply to wring out of the natives a hundred or two hundred thousand pounds as speedily as possible, that he might return home before his constitution had suffered from the heat to marry a peer's daughter, to buy rotten boroughs in Cornwall, to give balls in St. James's Square." So wrote Lord Macaulay in his essay on Warren Hastings, adding, "At first English power came among Indians unaccompanied by English morality." The Directors exhorted Hastings, whom they appointed Governor of Bengal, "to govern leniently and send more money, practise strict justice and moderation . . . and send more money."

To placate his London masters, Hastings sold Allahabad and Corah to the Prince of Oudh for half a million sterling. In these modern days, with political leaders preaching self-determination and denouncing the transference of peoples like goods and chattels from one State to another, this lapse in conduct on the part of Hastings seems most reprehensible, but it was child's play in the calendar of crime to the loan of British imperial troops to the same rapacious prince for the sum of £400,000 in order that he might engage in war without provocation for the purpose of slaughtering the Rohillas and appropriating their lands. After the British defeated the Rohillas in battle Macaulay relates that "the horrors of Indian war were let loose in the fair villages and cities of Rohilcund. The whole country was in a blaze. More than 100,000 people fled their homes to pestilential jungles, preferring famine and fever and the haunts of tigers to the tyranny of him to whom an English and a Christian Government had, for shameful lucre, sold their substance and their blood and the honour of their wives and daughters."

Macaulay, in his essay on Lord Clive, wrote: "He descended without scruple to falsehood, to hypocritical caresses, to the substitution of documents, and to the counterfeiting of hands. . . . He forged Admiral Watson's name;" and regarding Clive's breach of faith with Omichand, "As we think that breach of faith not only unnecessary, but most inexpedient, we need hardly say that we altogether condemn it."

In the same essay Macaulay relates how the East India Company received £800,000 out of the coffers of Bengal, after the battle of Plassey, from the puppet—Meer Jaffier—whom Clive placed on the throne of Bengal after the defeat and murder of Surajah Dowlah. "The Treasury of Bengal was thrown open to Clive," and "he accepted between two and three hundred thousand pounds." "The whole of this splendid estate (lands to the south of Calcutta bringing in nearly £30,000 sterling a year), sufficient to support with dignity the highest rank of the British peerage, was now conferred on Clive for life" by his puppet Meer Jaffier. "The pecuniary transactions between Meer Jaffier and Clive were sixteen years later condemned by the public voice and severely criticised in Parliament," when Clive in his own defence exclaimed, "By God, Mr. Chairman, at this moment I stand astonished at my own moderation!"

Clive and Warren Hastings, with thousands of minor British satellites, did for modern India what Attila and the Huns did for ancient Rome, and the British Parliament put up a statue to Clive in proximity to the India Office to mark for all time their appreciation of this exemplar of British vandalism.

This illegitimate and indiscriminate "bleeding" of India—to use Lord Salisbury's famous expression—went on for more than a hundred years under the domination of the East India Company, with the moral and national support of the British Parliament, until at length the dignity of Parliament and the British conscience could stand it no longer, when India was transferred to the tender mercy of the British crown.

Under the Crown the "bleeding" continued, only less copiously, less openly, and less indiscriminately, regularised and systematised and camouflaged by "services rendered" in return. Lord Salisbury, as Secretary of State for India, recognised it when he said: "As India must be bled, the lancet should be directed to the parts where the blood is congested, or at least is sufficient, not to those (the agricultural people) which are already feeble for the want of it."

In the good old days of the Company—good for England and bad for India—when the Company had a monopoly of trade, the rulers of India were merchants first and foremost and rulers second and hindmost, doing a little profiteering on their own account and bigger profiteering for the Company. Viceroys like Warren Hastings bought wheat, jute, tea, etc., at low rates, sometimes enforced rates, with a pre-emption of produce which the Company had imposed on the ryot, signed bills of lading, and despatched the goods to the India Office in London to pay dividends to the shareholders, and interest and capital to the British Government for the hire of troops which the Company employed to kill Indians and to appropriate their territories. This barbaric and crude method of bleeding India was changed by the Crown for a more civilised and scientific method, called Capitalism, in which the civil and military rulers were debarred from being glorified merchants, but received honourable and handsome pay from Indians for keeping law and order, while the capitalists made hay by exploiting

Indians at starvation wages and by exploiting the resources of India for the benefit of England.

India is far and away the best "investment" England has ever made, and little do the English people know how many of their countrymen are rolling in wealth at India's expense.

I have dwelt at some length upon Swaraj as the first and essential remedy for Indian poverty and for the low standard of Indian life because of the national bias of British rulers to govern India in the interests of themselves and their country, a bias common to all conquerors in their treatment of subject races, and a bias so honestly acknowledged by Sir John Strachey. I must now dwell upon the necessity of the government of India by Indians in order to effect all the other remedies for poverty, unemployment and an impoverished level of living.

Let me enumerate the leading remedies and palliatives: improvement and development and nationalisation, *if need be*, of education, agriculture and industry, including electrification, irrigation, railways, etc.; Indianisation of the administration and army; economisation on the army and administration; Swadeshi; extension of trade unions and linking up with international trade unions; inauguration of a poor law system, old age pensions, pensions for widows, national health insurance, etc., a minimum wage and trade boards; raising the age of marriage; restriction of the population by birth control; prohibition of the manufacture and sale of alcoholic beverages, and of opium except for medicinal and scientific purposes; regulation of the hours of labour and of child labour; emigration, etc.

I have given the first place to education because

improvement and development of man, mind and body, must precede the improvement and development of agriculture, of industry, and of the defensive forces against both external and internal enemies, against natural enemies like ignorance, drought and disease, and unnatural enemies like Capitalists and Imperialists. As I shall show in the chapter on education, Great Britain has ignored and neglected her first duty to India, namely, the education of the masses.

A firm believer in the principle of direct taxation, and definitely opposed to all taxation of the poor (except for luxuries like intoxicants and tobacco) on moral, economic and health grounds, believing also that tariffs make the rich richer and the poor poorer, and that tariff wars between nations are disastrous to international trade and international fellowship, I am of the opinion that India's economic salvation lies in the nationalisation of her agriculture and industries under a national Government. I must emphasise the government of India by Indians because "the trail of finance" is over the whole history of India since the first day of the British occupation until the present time. Human nature being what it is, as Lord Balfour would say, it is not to be expected otherwise. But, lest I am charged with exaggeration, let me cite two modern instances.

First, the Government of India (Civil Servants) Act, which was passed by both Houses of the British Parliament in 1925, adopted the chief recommendations of the Lee Commission—popularly or unpopularly known in India as the "Loot Commission"—namely, removing from the votes the salaries and pensions of superior persons, almost all British, in the hierarchy of the Indian Civil Service, the granting of pay, first-class passages to and from India, and other concessions, amounting to over £1,000,000 per annum, forming a considerable drain on India's slender resources.

The Lee benefits have been extended by the Government of India, with the sanction of the Government of England, to the higher officials, mostly British, in the railway service in spite of an adverse vote of the Assembly.

This financial interference of the British Parliament in the affairs of India is open to grave criticism, if not severe censure, because the All India Legislative Assembly turned down the Lee Report by sixty-eight votes to forty-six in the preceding year.

By way of comment upon this Act to bleed India without India's consent, would the Canadian, or Australian, or South African, or Irish Parliament brook such interference by the Imperial Parliament without cutting the painter? Why do British Imperialists rage, and their press spit fire at Indian patriots who "walk out" of these whited sepulchres, painted to look like parliaments, and who decline to co-operate with their captors and exploiters, and to be fooled by the paramount Power?

The second citation belongs to a different category, but one involving the honour and reputation of England and of the Church of England by law established. The "demand for grant" for the Church of England in the Indian Budget for 1925–26 amounted to 33,88,000 rupees (almost 34 lakhs, equal to nearly £226,000). Instead of being a decrease, this marks an increase of 10 lakhs on the Budget for 1924–25. This "demand" is non-votable by the Legislative Assembly. Reduced to plain English, the Church of England in India, with the consent of the Government of India and the Government of England, but without the consent of Indians, takes nearly a quarter of a million annually out of the depleted coffers of poor India, and in violation of Queen Victoria's pledge. The impropriety or immorality of this proceeding never seems to have occurred to the consciences, warped and scarred by Imperialism, of the bishops and archbishops responsible for the morals of the Church of England, or to the British Parliament, responsible for the international morals of England. When the Church of England, an alien Church in India, backed by an alien Government, exacts tribute to the tune of £226,000 per annum from the poorest people in the world without their permission, legal phraseology fails to fit the offence, and when the poor Indian villager asks the Indian Government for a free school for his children costing a few rupees per month, he is tartly told that there is money to increase the salaries of British officials and to subsidise the Church of England, one of the richest Churches in Christendom, but now there is none left in the national exchequer to educate the poor children. Truly the moral burden of the white man in India is heavy, and his sense of trusteeship past finding out. Truly is financial justice impossible in India under British rule. I leave the reader the disagreeable task of assessing the moral damage done to Christianity and British justice by this.

When will British Imperialists have the honesty and courage to recognise the great truth in Sir John Strachey's confession that no man can serve two masters, that no Englishman in the higher Civil Service in the bureaucracy, when it comes to a question of policy affecting the interests of England and India, can serve both England and India at the same time?

Needless to say that, when the choice has to be made, the vast majority of Englishmen serve England and betray India, although India pays the piper.

Morally how do such men stand?

When will Lord Birkenhead or any future Secretary of State for India have the honesty and courage to explain to every young aspirant for the Indian Civil Service that one day he will have to face the awful dilemma of choosing which master he will serve, the Indian one, who pays him, or the English one, who appoints, promotes, or dismisses him?

When will England have the honesty and courage to recognise that she cannot serve God and Mammon, that she is in a pharisaical position, an immoral position, as ruler of India, that Mammon has had a free hand in India under British rule to exploit and degrade and impoverish her vast population, and that Mammon and Mars together have done the things which they ought not to have done, and left undone those things which they ought to have done? Whenever England has had to choose between God and Mammon in her governance of India, she almost invariably has preferred Mammon.

When will the better England, the nobler England, the liberty-loving England, the England of Durham and Campbell-Bannerman, arise and give to India her precious and legitimate rights, self-government and freedom?

The extent of the blood-letting may be gathered from the study of the exports and imports in the Statistical Abstract for India, which shows a tremendous balance of exports over imports. For appreciation of this dismal science the reader will consult John Stuart Mill, who points out that exports and imports should equal each other, and that "tribute or remittances of rent to absentee landlords or of *interest to foreign creditors*" disturb this equality, and "the result is that a country which makes regular payments to foreign countries, *besides losing what it pays, loses also something more* by the less advantageous terms on which it is forced to exchange its productions for foreign commodities."

When Financial Member of the Government of India, Sir John Strachey declared: "India is a country of unbounded resources, but her people are a poor people. Its characteristics are great powers of production, but almost total absence of accumulated capital. On this account alone the prosperity of the country essentially depends on its being able to secure a large and favourable outlet for its surplus produce. But there is a special feature in the economic conditions of India which renders this a matter of yet more pressing and even of vital importance. This is the fact that her connection with England and the financial results of that connection compel her to send to Europe every year about £20,000,000 sterling worth of her products without receiving in return any direct commercial equivalent. This excess of exports over imports is really the return for the foreign capital, in its broadest sense, invested in India, including under capital, not only money, but all advantages which have to be paid for, such as the intelligence, strength and energy on which good administration and commercial prosperity depend. From these causes the trade of India is in an abnormal position, preventing her from receiving, in the shape of imported merchandise and treasure, the full commercial benefit which otherwise would spring from her vast material resources. . . . Here, then, is a country which both from its poverty, the primitive and monotonous condition of its industrial life, and the peculiar character of its political condition, requires from its Government, before all things, the most economical treatment of its resources, and, therefore, the greatest possible freedom in its foreign exchanges."

This frank and honest avowal of Sir John Strachey fixes the loss to India from the British connection at £20,000,000 a year, which during the course of British rule, extending over a hundred years, must mount up to thousands of millions. His compensation for this financial drain in "good administration, etc.," will not reduce the pangs of hunger of the poor peasants and artisans, and will sound like mockery to the unemployed middle classes who ought to fill the higher posts in the administration of their country, occupied by "angels" from England at salaries and pensions which appear to Indians extraordinarily extravagant. The Marquis of Salisbury suggested no compensation when he drew attention to the fact that "much of the revenue of India is exported without a direct equivalent."

In speaking of the "almost total absence of accumulated capital" in India, Sir John did not say how far this was due to the poverty of the people, or to the habit of hoarding (inculcated partly by insecurity of private property under Mohammedan and British conquest, and partly by the joint family social institution), or to the dislocation of the exchanges and drain from British domination. So far as "hoarding" is concerned, Mr. Pillai writes: "There is reason to think that the hoarded wealth of India has generally been exaggerated"; and the information supplied to the Bengal National Chamber of Commerce proved that "the ryots in Bengal at least have no hoard," and "whatever silver and gold ornaments they have are not worth taking notice of," and "if there had been a hoard the Government would not have provided money to the ryots on the first sign of famine in order to keep them alive."

Whatever the explanation may be, the fact remains that foreign capital dominates Indian industries, aggregating approximately £570,000,000 in 1917–18, of which £470,000,000 was calculated by the *Economist* in 1909 to be British. The distribution of the investments, according to Sir George Paish in 1910 and Mr. H. F. Howard in 1911, may be judged from the estimates given on p. 123.

The advantages and disadvantages of capital open up a wide sea of tempestuous propositions, both economic and political, which can only be summarily dealt with here.

To take the political, as the more vital, first. The history of the world in general and of India in particular teaches the danger of "economic penetration" of one country by another, leading too often to "political penetration" and loss of political and economic liberty.

This is the history of Africa, with the exception of Abyssinia, which retains a precarious independence.

It is the history of Asia, where the European vultures, fortunately for Asia and the world, met with more than a pin-prick from Japan, which has become the rallying ground for Asia to turn the European beasts of prey out of their continent. This does not mean that trade between Asia and Europe would cease, but simply that Asia would resume the political and economic freedom which has been wrenched from her by the sword of European capitalism.

FOREIGN INVESTMENTS IN INDIA

Sir George Paish (India and Ceylon together in thousands).

	£
Government	178,995
Municipal	3,522
Railways	136,519
Banks	3,400
Commercial and industrial	2,467
Electric light and power	1,763
Financial, land and investment	1,853
Gas and water	659
Iron, steel and coal	803
Mines	3,531
Motor traction and manufacturing	90
Oil	3,184
Rubber	4,610
Tea and coffee	19,644
Telegraphs and telephones	43
Tramways	4,136
Total	£365,399,000

Mr. H. F. Howard (India alone in millions).

	£
I. Government loans :—	
India sterling stock	170
Enforced rupee paper held in London	9
Rupee paper held in India by Europeans	31
II. Railway annuities	73
III. Loans of local bodies, taking the foreign share at less than three-tenths of the whole	10
IV. Companies registered in India, taking the foreign share at less than half of the whole	20
V. Companies with sterling capital carrying on business more or less exclusively in India :—	
Railway companies	77
Tea companies	13·5
Other companies	20·5
VI. Banking, loan, insurance, etc.	26
	£450,000,000

It is the history of China, which as we write is asserting her independence against foreign intervention.

It is the history of India, where the locusts of Europe from Portugal, Holland, Britain and France began nibbling bits of green, and then developed steel mandibles and bellies of belching fire, devouring and destroying all who opposed them, until finally the British species came out on top, binding India in a vice of political and economic slavery without parallel in the history of the world.

This tragedy, perhaps the greatest tragedy in history, the complete conquest of India and the political and economic subjection of 300 millions of human beings to the vampire of British capitalism, should make the British people observe one minute's silence every year in which to repent of the evil done in their name, and to undo it as far as it is possible by restoring India's freedom of action by responsible government.

For the Government of India to sanction more British investments directly in Indian industries would be to increase the hold of British capitalism, and probably to postpone the day of India's freedom, for capitalists' ideals of self-government are strictly limited to themselves.

Secondly, on the purely economic side, we must make a distinction between capital borrowed by Indians and capital directly employed in India by the foreigner. Money borrowed at low rates of interest from abroad for the development of railways other than strategic, and for irrigation and other useful works, is like "the gentle rain from heaven: it blesseth him that lends and him that takes." But when the British capitalist invests money in gold and coal mines, in jute mills and tea plantations, in India, the whole situation is changed,

India's resources being reduced and England's wealth increased.

The fundamental principle for every country, and for India, is that the profits of industry should remain in the country with the exception of a small charge for interest on any money borrowed from abroad.

The only advantage that India derives from British-owned industries is sweated wages and a low standard of life for Indian labour, a very dubious advantage which Indians might be better without, higher salaries being paid to the British management, and the dividends going to England.

Sir Thomas Holland warned India of the loss she suffers from the foreign exploitation of her minerals, taking the manganese industry as an illustration. "The whole output of 1892–1911, about four and a half million tons of high-grade ore, was exported, thus contributing to the economic development of other countries, while India received as compensation only a small fraction of the market value of the mineral. In this case the ore must have brought about eight millions sterling in the European market, but the Indian Government and the Indian States obtained only their royalty of about £56,000, while another portion of the estimated value was spent on labour and transport in India."

This brings us to the all-important question of State intervention and nationalisation or Socialism as the remedy for India's poverty and economic ills. Capitalism has failed in India, as it has failed in England, to give the working classes (whom Mill called the nation), whether they labour in the fields or in the towns, a fair wage, regularity of employment, and a decent standard of life. How egregiously capitalism has failed in India is writ large in the starvation wages, the general poverty, the chronicity of famine, the widespread unemployment, the bad housing, the prevalence of disease, the high death-rate, and the low average of life.

In modern times Governments as far afield as London and Tokyo have practised State Socialism and nationalisation of industry when necessity demanded. In other words, private initiative, private enterprise, private competition and exploitation of the public by capitalists, either in their individual or collective capacity, have been eliminated when the need became imperative; in short, State Socialism was their salvation when capitalism either failed or could no longer be trusted. During the Great War this was particularly true, and since the war Governments all the world over have been slowly, and too often reluctantly, compelled by economic experience to take a leading hand in the control and development of agriculture and industry, which are the first steps to nationalisation.

The attitude of the most Conservative Government of modern times towards the coal industry in Great Britain points the finger-post to nationalisation as the inevitable means of salvation of her key industry; and once coal goes, other industries are sure to follow. The Labour party, backed by an intelligent and awakened electorate, will see to that.

The needs of India cry aloud for nationalisation as the best means for development of her agricultural and other industries, without which she cannot find economic salvation. The great master of economic principles, John Stuart Mill, was evidently thinking of India when he wrote: " In the particular circumstances of a given age or nation there is scarcely anything really important to the general interest which it may not be desirable, or even necessary, that the Government should take upon itself, not because private individuals cannot effectively perform it, but because they will not. At some times and places there will be no roads, docks, harbours, canals, works of irrigation, hospitals, schools, colleges, printing presses, unless the Government establishes them, the public being either too poor to command the necessary resources, or too little advanced in intelligence to appreciate the end, or not sufficiently practised in conjoint action to be capable of the means. This is true, more or less, of all countries inured to despotism, and particularly of those in which there is a very wide distance in civilisation between the people and the Government, as of those which have been conquered and are retained in subjection by a more energetic and more cultivated people."

Briefly and chronologically let us trace the policy of the Government of India towards industry.

From 1757 to 1833 Government actively engaged in organising and financing industry, as we have already seen, for the benefit of its members and the shareholders in the East India Company; Professor C. J. Hamilton summarised this period :—

" In various parts of the country the East India Company maintained subordinate factories, and each of these had its local branches supervising production in the area around it. In each such area the Company employed a Gomasthah (agent) through whom contracts for the supply of cloths, etc., were made with the weavers, and advances of money for the purchase of raw materials arranged in order to see that the weavers did not sell their work to outsiders who offered higher prices; peons were appointed to supervise them; and the Company also had its own inspectors to certify to the quality of the cloth produced. The weavers complained that these agents abused their authority and forced them to accept non-remunerative wages. It will be seen that there was in this system room for the Company and its agents to force the weavers to accept advances and then compel them to surrender their cloths at unduly low prices, or to suffer at the hands of the peons, while there was equally the real danger that in the absence of strict supervision the Company might suffer heavy losses by making advances for which it got nothing in return, or by having to accept goods of very inferior quality."

In 1833 the monopoly of the East India Company was abolished by Parliament at the instigation of British manufacturers, jealous of its privileges and anxious to have a share in the Indian spoils; and from 1833 to 1857 the Indian cow became subject to milking conjointly by the Government of India through the Company and by the general body of British manufacturers.

With the transference of India to the Crown in 1857 the iniquitous system of Company rule ended, and the Government of India assumed a double *rôle*, that of trying to serve two masters at the same time, England and India, an improvement upon Company rule, which served only one master, itself. In fairness to the Directors of the East India Company, whose shades are to be seen flitting restlessly in Inferno, it ought to be stated that they made a death-bed repentance under Lord Dalhousie's stimulus by creating in 1854 the Department of Public Works, and by commencing the construction of roads, railways and irrigation canals. From a greedy, consuming and cankerous despotism the government of India passed under the Crown to a bureaucratic despotism relieved by lucid intervals of benevolence and intelligence and consideration for Indian interests.

Without sufficient courage to build the railways itself, the Government guaranteed a minimum return of 5 per cent. on the capital expended by private companies. Now all the railways are national property and almost all of them worked by the Government.

The *laissez-faire* attitude of the Government towards indigenous industries was spurred by famine and by the recommendations of the Famine Commission of 1880 that " the inception of new industries was the best palliative for famine, and that the Government ought to pioneer the manufacture and refining of sugar, the tanning of hides, the manufacture of fabrics of cotton, wool, silk, the preparation of fibres of other sorts and of tobacco, and the manufacture of paper, pottery, glass, soap and candles." The Commissioners drew attention to the " success of Government establishments, such as the tannery at Cawnpore, which largely supplies harness for the army, and the carpet and other manufactures carried on in some of the larger gaols," to the value of these as " schools for training the people of the country in improved methods," and " to their power to attract labour which would otherwise be employed to comparatively little purpose on the land, and thus set up a new bulwark against the total prostration of the labour market, which, in the present condition of the population, follows on every severe drought."

The Government trifled with these comprehensive

recommendations until 1898, when Sir Alfred Chatterton, Superintendent of the Madras School of Arts, obtained a small grant from the Government for experiments in the manufacture of aluminium vessels, which rapidly developed into a successful business, with the creation of more factories in other parts of India. This conspicuous success in State Socialism, which Sir Alfred pushed in other industries besides aluminium, like chromo-tanning, hand-loom weaving, etc., alarmed the English exploiters in India, who evidently brought sufficient pressure to bear upon the Government to constrain it to sell its factories to the Indian Aluminium Company in 1903. Impressed by the need and possibility of direct action on the part of the Government in the industrialisation of India, Lord Curzon in 1905 initiated the Imperial Department of Commerce and Industry under a Director of Industries, assisted by a committee of officials and business men, whose chief duties were "to be the dissemination of industrial information, the introduction of new, and the stimulation of existing, industries." In 1910 Lord Morley, the Secretary of State for India, put on the cold douche: "The policy which I am prepared to sanction is that State funds may be expended upon familiarising the people with such improvements in the methods of production as modern science and the practice of European countries can suggest; further than this the State should not go, and it must be left to private enterprise to demonstrate that these improvements can be adopted with commercial advantage." Two years later Lord Morley's successor at the India Office, Lord Crewe, favoured "the purchase and maintenance of experimental plant for the purpose of demonstrating the advantages of improved machinery or new processes and for ascertaining the data of production."

The war forced the pace, and in April, 1917, the Indian Munitions Board was formed and commenced to work successfully. Its experiments in manufacturing on a large scale, as well as in administration, enabled the Industrial Commission to arrive practically at the same conclusions as those formulated by the Famine Commission of 1880: (1) "that in future Government must play an active part in the industrial development of the country, and (2) that it is impossible for Government to undertake that part unless provided with adequate administrative equipment and forearmed with reliable scientific and technical advice."

In 1919 the Joint Select Committee on the Government of India Bill reported: "Whatever may be the right fiscal policy for India, for the need of her consumers as well as for her manufacturers, it is quite clear that she should have the same liberty to consider her interests as Great Britain, Australia, New Zealand, Canada and South Africa. In the opinion of the Committee, therefore, the Secretary of State should, as far as possible, avoid interference on this subject when the Government of India and its legislature are in agreement." This principle of full fiscal autonomy for India was accepted by the Secretary of State on June 30th, 1921.

Into the pros and cons of Free Trade and Protection for India the writer dares not presume to travel, as being too vast and too involved, and demanding a special treatise. Besides, he is a convinced Free Trader and a convinced Home Ruler, but as a Home Ruler feels precluded from discussing fiscal policy, which ought to be decided by Indians in the complete enjoyment of Swaraj. Political expediency, however, did drive the Government during the war into a policy of practical Protection, when the increased expenditure was met by increasing the customs revenue, the Government dreading the unpopularity attached to direct taxation. Instead of placing the burden of the war upon the backs of the direct taxpayers, the Government of India shovelled it on to those of the rich and poor without any discrimination in favour of the poor. In 1916 import duties were raised from 5 to 7·5 per cent., in 1921 to 11 per cent. to balance the deficit of 6 crores, and in 1922 to 15 per cent. to meet the deficit of 90 crores in the national Budget.

To those readers who are interested in Fiscal Policy, I commend a study of works on the subject in general, and of "The Indian Steel Industries (Protection) Act, 1924," and of "The History of the Tata Iron and Steel Company" in particular.

CHAPTER VI

AGRICULTURE AND THE REMEDY FOR POVERTY

"FOR generations to come the progress of India in wealth and civilisation must be directly dependent on her progress in agriculture. There is, perhaps, no country in the world in which the State has so immediate and direct an interest in agriculture. The Government of India is not only a Government, but the chief landlord. The land revenue is derived from that portion of the rent which belongs to the State, and not to individual proprietors. Throughout the greater part of India every measure for the improvement of the land enhances the value of the property of the State. The duties which in England are performed by a good landlord fall in India in a great measure upon the Government. Speaking generally, the only Indian landlord who can command the requisite capital and knowledge is the State." When Lord Mayo penned these lines in 1869 he exhibited not only the knowledge of a practical agriculturist, but the mind of a great statesman and the heart of a humanitarian, who saw in the nationalisation of the land the salvation of India's poverty-stricken millions, nine-tenths of whom find their livelihood in agriculture. Under his inspiration a "Department of Agriculture, Revenue and Commerce" was initiated in the following year, with Mr. Hume, whose friendship I cherished, as secretary. Short and sad was its existence, for the Secretary of State in London, probably fearing the taint of nationalisation, and caring nothing for India's myriads, immediately transformed it into a Revenue Department, and in 1879 it was actually re-absorbed in the Home Department.

Here endeth the first chapter of British official indifference to India's chief source of "progress." The second chapter begins with the resuscitation in 1881 of the recommendation of the Famine Commission of Central and Provincial Departments of Land Records and Agriculture, but during the next twenty years the departments did little or nothing, and that very unwisely, for agriculture, and a lot for dry-as-dust records.

The third chapter opens in the early years of this century with the reorganisation of the Agricultural Department, its separation from land records, and the appointment of an Inspector-General of Agriculture to secure co-ordination and co-operation throughout India. Mr. J. McKenna summed up the situation as follows: "Such were the beginnings of agricultural policy—if it can be called a policy. Early endeavours were too ambitious, and the machinery—a centralised secretariat—was imperfect. The object aimed at was to increase the revenues of India by the improvement of agriculture, but nothing was done for that improvement, and the expansion of the land records staff and the compilation of statistics almost entirely occupied the attention of the provincial departments. But the foundations had been laid, and the next few years were to witness a rapid development."

Agricultural colleges sprang up at Pusa, Poona, Cawnpore, Salem, Lyallpur and Coimbatore, and veterinary colleges at Bombay, Lahore, Calcutta and Madras, and a bacteriological laboratory at Muktesar. The Government carried on seed farms, demonstration farms and implement depots. Ocular demonstrations of new methods, combining scientific with practical knowledge, were given in many places for the benefit of the ryots.

Tillage, which forms such a vital part of farming, has been improved, although the primitive plough—a wooden stick with a small iron point—which merely scratches the ground, is still in general use, largely because the cattle are not strong enough, owing to insufficient fodder, to draw a heavier plough. Irrigation, as we noted when discussing famine, has been greatly increased. The total area under irrigation in 1920 was nearly 49,000,000 acres, of which 20,550,000 were irrigated from Government canals, 2,647,000 from private canals, 7,337,000 from tanks, 12,692,000 from wells, and 5,737,000 from other sources. The £51,447,375 spent by the Government on irrigation yielded a profit of nearly £2,275,000 to the State after payment of interest charges, besides increasing the fertility of the soil and the number and richness of the crops, and thus helping the cultivators.

Manure, as an aid to tillage, is difficult to obtain, because of the poverty of the peasants, who cannot afford to buy artificial manures, and use cattle manure, dried in the sun in the form of cakes, called " varalties," for household fires, instead of for the land, which custom could be avoided by supplying the peasants with cheap firewood. The utilisation of night-soil as manure, which has been such a success in other countries like Holland, Germany and Japan, has hardly been adopted at all in India, this natural fertiliser being allowed to fester on village sites as a nuisance. The same applies to bones of dead animals, most valuable fertilisers, which accumulate as Golgothas outside the villages.

The provision of village schools by the Government, with the teaching of elementary agricultural science, would change this backwardness in farming, which is so much due to ignorance, and the schoolmaster would be the intellectual and material benefactor of the poor ryot.

In the fearful struggle for existence cattle are the needful friends of the peasants, ploughing, raising water from the wells, threshing, carrying produce, working oil mills, supplying manure, and last, but not least, providing milk, the best food for man, woman and child, which is all the more valuable in India owing to the vegetarian habits of the people. Like their masters, cattle suffer from poverty, underfeeding, famine and disease, all avoidable to a large extent, if the great landlord, the Government, put its back and intelligence into the matter by providing sufficient grazing land and more veterinary surgeons and dispensaries for the 146 millions of cattle in the country.

In order to enable the reader to better grasp the urgency of the need to improve cultivation of the soil in India, I submit the following statement made by Mr. Martin, Census Commissioner for India, at the Royal Society of Arts, in 1923: "The problem of the pressure of population on food and wealth production is one which is receiving more and more serious consideration at the hands of Indian economists. There are many obstacles in the way of improvement in conditions of cultivation: the ignorance, immobility and conservatism of the agricultural population, the system of land tenure with its progressive fragmentation of holdings, and the difficulties connected with the introduction of agricultural machinery. Yet industrial development, even if it be possible on a large scale in

India, cannot take the place of agriculture. The country must produce food for an increasing population or become dependent on the world's food supplies, with disastrous consequences. We have had in the last few years the new phenomenon of an import of wheat in India from Australia. India requires much more from outside for her development, and she must depend for many years on what she produces from the ground to pay for what she must get from other countries."

Further, to make sure of our ground in combating poverty and procuring food for the people, the interdependence of agriculture and industry must be clearly understood. Improvement and increased production in agriculture is essential to improvement and increased production in industry. How can industry prosper when large masses of the agricultural population are too poor to buy its products, not to mention their low standard of life and few wants? And how can agriculture prosper unless industry prospers and provides alternative employment to the agriculturist, who, with his average of two to three acres, is unemployed 215 days in the year? An improvement in the quality and quantity of agricultural products, like cotton, and jute, and sugar-cane, and oil seeds, etc., means prosperity in the industries of which these form the raw materials. These are fundamentals which British rulers paid too little heed to during a hundred and fifty years.

Now for the obstacle of "land tenure with its progressive fragmentation of holdings," which may well be introduced by reproducing Mr. Pillai's classification of rural society in 1911 in British India as follows:—

Landlords, eight millions (principals and dependents).

Persons cultivating their own or rented land, 167 millions (principals and dependents).

Farm servants and field labourers, 41 millions (principals and dependents).

Estate agents, managers and their employees, one million (principals and dependents).

Total population supported by ordinary cultivation, 217 millions.

As we said before, the Government—the British Government in India—is the great landlord, having the first claim on the land, the revenue for which in 1923 amounted to 36 crores, and formed 18 per cent. of India's total revenue, in comparison with the 1 per cent. from land taxes in Great Britain. By too many Indians the land revenue is considered excessive, and a serious, if not the main, cause of agricultural depression and hindrance to agricultural improvement, the Government thereby failing in its duty as a landlord.

The consequences of high assessments for land revenue by the Government are, in the words of the Hon. G. K. Parekh, M.L.C.—

"(*a*) that the agriculturist is obliged to borrow;

"(*b*) that he is unable to manure the land properly;

"(*c*) that he is prevented from keeping his lands fallow or from having a proper rotation of crops, and is obliged to utilise all his lands for the crop that pays him best, quite irrespective of its effect in impoverishing the land."

As the Government claims the uncultivated land as well as the cultivated, the responsibility resting upon its shoulders for bringing waste lands under cultivation, and thus developing the economic resources of the country and increasing the food supply, must not be overlooked in considering the remedies for poverty and unemployment. Quoting Sir John Strachey, "exclusive of Bengal, for which there are no statistics, there are said to be in India some 80,000,000 acres of unoccupied land fit for cultivation—an area exceeding the whole area of the United Kingdom."

Agricultural figures for British India, excluding Indian States, for 1919–20 are—

	Acres.	Percentage of Total Area.
Forests	88,323,000	14
Not available for cultivation .	145,770,000	23
Culturable waste other than fallow	113,415,000	18
Current fallows . . .	52,135,000	9
Net sown area . . .	222,825,000	36
Total . . .	622,468,000	100

Anent these figures the following questions arise :—

1. Does not the cultivation of this vast area of 113,000,000 acres of unoccupied land fit for cultivation provide one of the most natural and effective remedies for poverty and unemployment ?

2. Why has the British bureaucracy neglected or made so little use of this remedy ?

3. Would it not be in accordance with every principle of righteousness and justice to allow a Government of Indians to grapple with this gigantic problem, India's most gigantic problem ?

The bureaucrat's reply to the second question would probably be, " It is not profitable to do so," therein betraying his proverbial short-sightedness and lack of statesmanship.

To reclaim waste lands or lands reserved for the pleasure of the rich—hunting, shooting, wild game, etc.—whether in Australia, Canada, England or India, is seldom a paying proposition at first, but after many days of toil and struggle the fruit of man's fortitude glows in golden grain, bringing health and strength and happiness to millions. How much better for India's future, for the raising of India's distressed and impoverished people, if the Government sank millions of money in cultivating the present inhospitable tracts of land instead of in building Imperial Delhi and in maintaining colossal armaments!

The progressive fragmentation of land is due to the ancient Hindu law of inheritance by which each child receives a part of every plot owned by the deceased. The evil effects of excessive subdivision of land involve interference with cultivation, prevention of permanent improvement and orderly organisation of labour and capital, and waste of time. Mr. Keatinge mentions one village in the Kanara district where 52 acres of land were held by 50 landholders in as many as 139 different plots, and Dr. Mann tells of a village in the Bombay Presidency in which 16 out of 156 landholders had their land divided into ten or more separate plots, some of them only a thirtieth of an acre.

The chief varieties of tenure are Zemindari and Ryotwari and, to a much smaller extent, Communal.

In the Zemindari system, which prevails in Northern India and which covers 53 per cent. of the land in British India, large landowners, called Zemindars or Talukdars, act as intermediaries between the Government and the cultivator, from whom they receive rent in cash or in a share of the produce, and they pay a share of this rent as land revenue to the Government.

The share paid to the Government is known as a "settlement," which is either "permanent" or "temporary." According to the permanent settlement, made in 1793, the Zemindars were at first assessed at 90 per cent. of what they collected from the cultivator, which amounted in 1854 to 50 per cent. and now to about 27 per cent., owing to improved conditions of assessment and in some cases to increased productivity. In the temporary settlement lands are assessed periodically, and the Zemindars pay half of what they receive from the tenants to the Government. Under the Zemindari system 27·1 per cent. of the land is settled permanently and 72·9 per cent. temporarily.

In the Ryotwari system, which prevails in the Provinces of Bombay, Madras and Punjab, the ryots, or peasant proprietors, hold their land direct from the Government under assessments made for thirty years. The Survey Department makes an estimate of the average annual value of the produce of every field, and after deducting the cost of cultivation and making allowances for vicissitudes of seasons, distance of markets, etc., fixes one-half of the net profit as the share of the Government, which works out at between 6 and 7 per cent. of the gross produce.

In the Communal system, which is a *rara avis* nowadays, the village is jointly responsible for payment of land revenue to the Government. The Famine Commissioners of 1880 reported that "these village communities are represented by an elected or hereditary headman and are jointly responsible for the payment of the Government revenue due from the entire village. Sometimes all the land is held in common, and the proceeds are thrown together and divided among the sharers by village custom. Sometimes the proprietors all have their separate holdings in the estate, each paying the quota of revenue due from his plot, and enjoying the surplus profits from it."

As it is impossible in the compass of this book to examine in detail these systems and the economic development of the country, we must confine ourselves to one or two general criticisms :—

Firstly, that the cultivator is taxed too heavily by both the superior landlord, the Government, and the inferior landlord, the Zemindar ; and secondly, that in consequence the cultivator is driven into debt to money-lenders, and improvement in agriculture rendered extremely difficult, if not impossible.

Having already dealt with the Government as landlord, it only remains to relate that the Zemindars, who own large estates, take advantage of the ignorant and resourceless peasantry by exacting high rents and more than their share of the produce of the land, in spite of the Bengal Rent Act of 1859, the Bengal Tenancy Act of 1885, and similar Acts in other Provinces for the regulation of relations between landlord and tenant, aiming at giving the tenant the desiderata of tenants throughout the world, namely, the three F's : fixity of tenure, fair rent, and full compensation for improvements. India, like Ireland, is cursed with too many landlords, who are mere rent-receivers and economic parasites, spending no money on land improvements and too often practising absenteeism.

These non-cultivating landlords, who are supported by agriculture, are a burden on the community, and, unfortunately, are on the increase. In Madras, for instance, they have increased from twenty in 1901 to seventy-seven in 1921 for every thousand workers (*i.e.*, excluding dependents).

The disease of debt, which is so deep and widespread among the small Ryotwari peasant proprietors and the small tenant farmers under the Zemindari system, deserves more attention than we can give it. Mr. Darling, in "The Punjab Peasant in Prosperity and Debt," supplies these salient facts :—

1. Only 17 per cent. are free from debt ;

2. Net mortgage debt is not more than 40 per cent. of the whole ;

3. The average debt per *indebted* proprietor is 463 rupees ; and

4. Total debt represents twelve times the land revenue paid by all concerned, whether indebted or not.

The Punjab Famine Report of 1878–79 estimated that over 80 per cent. of the proprietors of the Punjab are in debt, thus supporting Mr. Darling's findings, and Mr Calvert, in his work "The Wealth and Welfare of the Punjab," discovered 40,000 money-lenders in the Punjab out of a population of 25 millions.

Sir Frederick Nicholson estimated the total debt of the rural population in the Madras Presidency in 1895 at 45 crores, which worked out at an average of 13 rupees per head of the population. The Famine Commission of 1901 found that at least one-fourth of the cultivators of the Bombay Presidency have lost possession of their lands, that less than a fifth are free from debt, and that the remainder are indebted to a greater or less extent. The Material and Moral Progress Report for 1919 aggregated the indebtedness of the Punjab at about 30 millions sterling.

The speed at which the money-lenders have expropriated the peasantry may be judged by the following figures from the Punjab: From 1866 to 1874 sales averaged about 88,000 acres a year, and in the subsequent quinquennial periods 93,000, 160,000, 310,000, and 338,000 acres a year.

The rate of interest charged by these leeches varies from 15 to 50 per cent. compound interest. But yet the tale of expropriation is not all told, for the sowcar (money-lender) has taken advantage of the indebtedness, unbusinesslikeness, commercial helplessness, and ignorance of the cultivator by combining the business of grain merchant with that of money-lender, buying the ryot's harvest at low prices when there is a glut in the market and selling to the big exporter, who prefers to buy in bulk from him rather than from the individual cultivator, who can only sell in small quantities. The money-lender thus becomes the economic dictator of the village, monopolising the position of buyer and lender, exacting his own terms, and leaving only an infinitesimal part of the profits to the producers.

Regarding this unholy and uneconomic state of affairs, Mr. Darling sums it up in the following words: "The money-lender is everywhere the evil genius of the cultivator, exploiting him when he is prosperous and enslaving him when he is poor. . . . Economic freedom is a condition precedent to progress, and to the Indian cultivator no freedom is possible till the power of the money-lender is broken."

Before proceeding to a discussion of the remedies for these evils we must say one more word about the 41 millions of landless farm servants and field labourers, the flotsam and jetsam of agriculture, to whose terrible plight in life references have been made previously. The one more word here had better be in a summary of their sorrows, of "the slings and arrows of outrageous fortune," viz.:—low wages; the failure of wages to overtake prices; long hours; low productivity, the result of underfeeding and consequent weakness; unemployment during five or six months in the year; famine; disease and epidemics; economic slavery; insanitary housing, etc., if "housing" can be justly applied to the hovels in which they are herded.

Given the vote, what a beneficial change would come over the wretched lot of these unfortunate outcasts and helots of society! Their "untouchability" would immediately vanish; they would become citizens with equal rights, and, being citizens with a vote, they would command the attention of the Government and the Legislatures, their hard conditions would be relieved, and, best of all, their self-respect, self-reliance, and self-expression would be restored, to their own and their country's good.

Comparing the Punjab with the rest of India, Mr. Darling gives the following:—

Date.	District.	Percentage free from Debt.
1874	Central Provinces . .	60
1888	The tenantry in the Agrá district . . .	22
1894	Nagpur (18,000 tenants) .	40
1901	Baroda State . . .	40 (of all landowners)
1907	Faridpur (Bengal) . .	55 (of all cultivators)
1919	Mysore State (24,350 co-operators) . . .	37

The same careful investigator estimated the total rural debt of British India, with its population of 247 millions, at more than £400,000,000.

The Government and Redemption of Agriculture

Many of the remedies for agricultural backwardness and depression have been discussed already as they arose. For the sake of comprehensiveness, it might be as well to enumerate these, and then deal with those which have not yet been considered :—

(i.) Political : (*a*) self-government ; (*b*) adult suffrage.

(ii.) Education : primary, scientific, agricultural, industrial, technical, etc.

(iii.) Industrial : initiation of new industries and development of old industries.

(iv.) Agriculture.

(*a*) More Scientific Research Departments and more Agricultural Colleges for the improvement of the soil and crops and the prevention of pests and diseases, etc. ; more Veterinary Colleges and veterinary surgeons ; breeding of cattle and sheep demonstration farms ; a school in every village with teaching of agriculture, etc.

(*b*) Cultivation of waste lands fit for cultivation.

(*c*) Irrigation and still more irrigation.

(*d*) Co-operative societies.

(*e*) Agricultural banks and a national bank.

(*f*) Development of village industries.

(*g*) Restrictive legislation regarding money-lenders and alienation of the land, etc.

(*h*) Building and improvement of village roads for the purpose of transport, etc.

(*i*) Nationalisation of the land and its mineral resources, with reductions of assessments till nationalisation is attained.

(v.) Drastic reduction of military expenditure and armaments and wise and bold expenditure on agriculture.

Almost all these subjects have been treated more or less, except co-operation, banking, village industries, and restrictive legislation.

Co-operation

Co-operation is both an alleviative and curative remedy for the cardinal defects of Indian husbandry by providing the credit necessary for agriculture on reasonable terms and by organising the marketing of agricultural produce; in other words, by delivering the cultivator out of the clutches of the sowcar, both as money-lender and middle-man. Under Act X. of 1904 co-operation credit societies started their useful career, reaching 8,177 in number in 1911, with a membership of 403,318 and a capital of 33,500,000 rupees. In 1912 the Co-operative Societies Act II. widened their scope; and in 1921–22 their number rose to 52,182, with a membership of nearly two millions and a capital of 311,250,000 rupees. In 1925 the societies numbered 56,000.

The saving reaped by the peasantry on every crore of rupees lent by these societies was estimated by Sir E. Maclagan at 10 lakhs of rupees at least. After ten years' working in the Punjab 38 per cent. of the members were entirely free from debt, and the total indebtedness of the members had been reduced by £100,000. With loans from co-operative banks at

9 to 12½ per cent. instead of anything up to 75 per cent. from money-lenders, these figures can be appreciated.

In 1919 the total number of co-operative purchase, sale and productive societies, which are offshoots of the co-operative credit societies, was only 597, with 34,674 members and a working capital of 2,000,000 rupees.

Other national advantages derived from co-operation besides reduction of debt and credit at low rates include "better business, better farming and better living," better agricultural implements, planting of trees for timber in the future, repairing of the village wells, grants for sanitary improvements, building of meeting places, and consolidation of small holdings—"a real revolution, of incalculable benefit to the cultivators."

The moral progress arising out of co-operation may not be so easily measured as the material progress, but close observers like Mr. Calvert and Mr. Darling see an increase in industriousness, thrift, self-reliance, and probity on the part of the members, a substitution of arbitration for litigation, and a more definite avoidance of drinking and gambling than amongst non-members.

Direct advances to the ryot out of national funds, in accordance with Acts passed in 1871, 1883 and 1884, were made by the Government for seed, cattle, land improvements, etc., but attained only trifling dimensions.

Restrictive legislation relating to debt, notably the Deccan Agriculturists' Relief Act of 1879 and Land Alienation Acts, applied to the Punjab, the United Provinces, and Bombay, did little to curtail the depredations of the money-lender upon the peasantry and to prevent the transfer of their lands to this species of ghoul. The money-lender, with his wit, always seems to be able to drive a bullock waggon through every Act of Parliament.

Less rigidity in the enforcement of the revenue demand and remittances of the Government's share in periods of bad crops reduced one of the causes driving the ryot into the deadly embrace of the sowcar.

These minor operations of the Government have set going tiny currents of the Gulf Stream which is needed to save the cultivators from the ocean of piratical money-lenders.

What India needs, and what India must have, for her economic salvation, is a major operation in the shape of effective nationalisation of the land, with the eradication of Zemindars, sowcars, and other exploiters of the cultivators. All other operations only lead up to this, and a wise surgeon performs the major operation before the patient's strength and recuperative powers are diminished or exhausted.

Land Nationalisation

Nationalisation of the land includes working its minerals for the benefit of the community and the nation instead of the foreign or Indian capitalist. Accompanying and complementing this land reform, the Government should provide agricultural banks and nationalise the Imperial Bank of India.

In comparison with these radical remedies for the redemption of India's agriculture, how futile, farcical and wasteful of time and money is the appointment of a Royal Commission on Agriculture without power to investigate the systems of land revenue and of land tenure, which form the root of the problem. This trifling on a grand scale with India's greatest problem is another manifestation, the latest manifestation, of incompetency on the part of Great Britain to rule India in her highest interests. The problem of Indian agriculture has been with us since the first day Britain entered India as a conqueror and ruler ; the floor of the India Office in Whitehall is littered with recommendations of Famine and other Commissions for the improvement and development of agriculture, and its shelves are packed with volumes written by English and Indian experts on agricultural resuscitation, and its innumerable vaults piled chock-a-block with reports, memoranda and monographs from the Department of Agriculture in India, with information and advice on this perennial problem ; but the great mind of the "steel frame" possesses neither the elasticity, nor the enterprise, nor the will, to undertake the real remedies for India's key industry.

India awaits with impatience the happy day when her affairs shall pass from the obstinate, self-satisfied and exploiting bureaucracy to a truly national Government, sympathetic and responsive to Indian public opinion, and bent on developing India's vast potentialities in field and mine and industry, and on making India the treasure-house of Indians, and no longer the exploiting ground of Britons.

Nationalisation of the land is not such a tall order as it may appear to some, for in theory the Government is the great owner of the land and minerals, and in practice to a large extent. All that is required is to make its ownership complete and perfect by eliminating the wasteful and harmful middle-man. Most of the irrigation canals are national property, likewise the railways, the Mint, the post and telegraph services, printing presses, forests, etc. India is ripe for nationalisation, for a Commonwealth of the people, but British rule, in league with British capitalism, blocks the way. Once more behold responsible self-government as the *sine quâ non* of India's regeneration.

Banks

The shortage of *banking facilities* in India handicaps both agriculture and industry. With a population of 319 millions, India had only 598 banking offices in 1921, while Canada, with a population of 8½ millions, had about 4,000 banks, and the United Kingdom, with a population of 48 millions, had 9,138 in 1917. In India 10·2 per cent. of the people live in towns of 5,000 or over inhabitants, and only 207 of these towns in 1921 possessed banks.

The organised banking systems of India comprise the Imperial Bank of India (an amalgamation of the Presidency banks of Bombay, Madras and Bengal), the exchange banks, which are chiefly concerned with financing trade at the seaports and towns, the Indian joint stock banks, the Post Office savings banks, and the co-operative banks.

Industrial and Fiscal Commissions and the External Capital Committee recommended the development of banking facilities for the employment of dormant Indian capital in Indian industries in place of British capital, but the Government of India took no active steps to carry out their recommendations, and in consequence British capitalism has had a roaring time in India. If the Imperial Bank of India had been nationalised by the Government, India would have been saved a serious financial drain in the past. For the present and future economic welfare of India nationalisation of her banking system is imperative, with full control over her currency and gold reserves, which have hitherto been subservient to London.

To be or not to be ? is the question. Has India to be sacrificed for ever on the altar of British high finance ? History answers, "Yes ! it is always so under foreign rule." Sir John Strachey answered, "Yes." British Imperialists say, "Yes," in the immoral jingle "My country, right or wrong." And the writer, who is only a student of psychology, replies, with Scottish caution, "Yes and no": "Yes !" as long as Liberals and Tories, tied to the chariot wheels of Capitalism, rule England and India ; "No !" when the British people realise that Imperialism and Capitalism are cursed things, and send a Labour Government to power with a mandate to give India political and financial self-government.

Indian financiers complain that the Government places all its revenues and reserves at the disposition of the Imperial Bank, which, in its turn, lends these Indian moneys to British traders and manufacturers, and thereby gives them an undue advantage in competition with Indian traders and manufacturers. Carried to its logical sequence, this means that a British Government uses Indian money to back Britons against Indians, hitting the Indian banks as well, because the Imperial Bank can lend money much more cheaply than the Indian banks owing to the fact that the Imperial Bank pays no interest to Government on its cash deposits and reserves. Another grievance against the Imperial Bank is that the bulk of the well-paid posts on its staffs are filled by Englishmen.

In respect to agricultural credit, it is of little avail for the Government to pass restrictive legislation on money-lenders unless they provide agricultural banks in the villages, for which Indian Nationalists have been clamouring for forty years.

Reverse Councils

The currency policy of the Government of India, especially between March, 1919, and September, 1920, has produced a crop of criticism on the part of Indian financiers. According to Mr. Moreton Frewen, England's indebtedness to India at that time amounted to 90 millions sterling, which, if paid in the normal way, would have meant a heavy drain on England's gold. The Secretary of State for India, therefore, resorted to the sale of Reverse Council bills, thus liquidating a large amount of the debt to the detriment of India.

The losses to India due to this policy were—

1. The low rate at which her sterling securities were sold and her sterling assets in London dissipated.
2. The liquidation of English debts owed to India with tremendous loss to India.
3. The heavy exodus of capital from India and a tight money market in India with a high rate for internal loans.
4. The decrease in India's national wealth owing to a fall in the price of securities of all kinds.
5. Foreign loans raised by the Government of India with a proportionate increase in home charges.
6. Indian companies being driven into bankruptcy owing to the high rate of interest.
7. The direct exchange loss of the Government of India, involving higher taxation.
8. The waste of national wealth by the artificial stimulus given to an unhealthy excess of imports over exports.

9. The effective prevention of the import of gold into India on the one hand and the encouragement of its export on the other.

It would not be easy to compute these losses to India, but Sir Montagu Webb estimated those due to the Reverse Councils sales in 1920 at £200,000,000 while Mr. Krishnamurti Iyer puts them at £300,000,000. On a moderate estimate the position can be summed up by saying that India's credit account of £90,000,000 sterling was converted into a debit of £110,000,000 by this Reverse Councils transaction.

Cottage Industries

Cottage industries have always played a useful and necessary part in the economic life of the people of India, and as far as one can foresee they will continue to do so both in the towns and villages. According to the last census 32½ millions of the population are distributed in 2,316 towns of 5,000 or more inhabitants, and 286½ millions in 685,655 villages.

The Census Report of 1911 reminds us: "Until the recent introduction of Western commodities, such as machine-made cloth, kerosene oil, umbrellas, and the like, each village was provided with a complete equipment of artisans and menials, and was thus almost wholly self-supporting and independent. . . . Where this system was fully developed, the duties and remuneration of each group of artisans were fixed by custom, and the caste rules strictly prohibited a man from entering into competition with another of the same caste. . . . They received a regular yearly payment for their services, which often took the form of a presumptive share of the harvest. . . . The village is no longer the self-contained industrial unit which it formerly was, and many disintegrating influences are at work to break down the solidarity of village life."

In spite of the competition of machine-made goods, whether manufactured in Europe or India, village industries are not dead yet, and must be fostered and increased as a second string to the agriculturist's bow, as a supplement and complement to the cultivation of the soil, which does not occupy his time for more than half the year, and which frequently fails from various causes, already discussed, to give him enough food to keep body and soul together.

The most important cottage industries are weaving and spinning, followed by tusser silk cultivation, bee-keeping, and the keeping of poultry, etc., towards the success of which co-operation is a vital factor. As we shall see in another chapter, Mahatma Gandhi pins his faith to the "charkha," the spinning-wheel, in every home as the sheet anchor of India's economic salvation.

The treatment of agriculture by the Government of India may be gleaned by the following comparative figures, supplied by Sir Henry Row in the *Edinburgh Review*, April, 1922:—

State Expenditure on Agriculture

Country.	Per 1,000 of Population.	Per 1,000 Acres of Total Area.	Per 1,000 Acres of Cultivated Area.
	£	£	£
United States of America (1919) .	68	4	14
Germany (1910) .	63	31	47
United Kingdom (1921)	64	65	92

In 1920–21 the total expenditure of the Government of India on agriculture amounted to £659,000 (£65,000 by the Imperial Department of Agriculture at Pusa and £594,000 by the Provincial Departments), which, according to *Moral and Material Progress of India* for 1922, works out at about ½*d*. per acre per annum.

Mr. Darling, in "The Punjab Peasant in Prosperity and Debt," converts Sir Henry Row's sterling figures at 15 rupees to the pound :—

	Per 1,000 of the Population.	Per 1,000 Acres (cultivated).
	Rupees.	Rupees.
Germany (1910) . .	945	705
United States (1919–20).	1,020	210
United Kingdom (1921)	960	1,380
Punjab (1921–22) . .	79	56

With regard to these figures Mr. Darling remarks : "No disparity in resources can entirely justify the contrast between the Punjab and the other three countries, especially when it is remembered that in 1921 England had a national debt of £8,000,000,000. No progress is possible without pecuniary sacrifice, and if the Punjab desires more rapid development it must be prepared to pay for it." And, I should like to add, if India desires more rapid development it must be prepared to pay for it by investing more money in agriculture.

When the military expenditure of upwards of £50,000,000 a year is compared with the £659,000 on agriculture one receives another picture of the mentality of British rulers in India. Against this comparison the capital outlay on irrigation works of 54 crores (roughly £40,000,000) up till 1924 has to be reckoned, but this expenditure brings in 7 to 8 per cent. interest to the Government, whose charges for water are deemed by the cultivators as too high and a serious impediment to agricultural improvement.

CHAPTER VII

INDIANISATION

INDIANISATION of the Civil and Military Services, with its moral, financial and political bearings, is indispensable to India's freedom and progress; it is also one of the remedies for India's poverty and unemployment.

This great principle was acknowledged and proclaimed by Act of Parliament in 1833: "And be it enacted that no native of the said territories (British India) nor any natural-born subject of His Majesty resident therein shall by reason only of his religion, place of birth, descent, colour, or any of them, be disabled from holding any place, office, or employment under the said Company," and again by Queen Victoria in 1858: "We hold ourselves bound to the natives of our Indian territories by the same obligations of duty which bind us to all our other subjects, and these obligations, by the blessing of Almighty God, we shall faithfully and conscientiously fulfil. It is our further will that, so far as may be, our subjects, of whatever race or creed, be freely and impartially admitted to offices in our service the duties of which they may be qualified by their education, ability, and integrity, duly to discharge."

With regard to these solemn pledges and promises, both the Duke of Argyll and Sir Stafford Northcote, in the capacity of Secretary of State for India, used the same words, namely, " We have not fulfilled our duty or the promises and engagements which we have made."

John Morley, as Secretary of State for India during 1906–10, may reasonably claim to be the first British statesman to have made the slightest success in overcoming the opposition of the British bureaucracy in India to redeeming these dishonoured and time-worn pledges when he appointed an Indian here and an Indian there into the official hierarchy.

Mr. Montagu's declaration of August 20th, 1917, in favour of responsible government, followed up by " The Government of India " Act, 1919, constituting a central and a provincial legislature, might be described by the innocent British spectator, jealous of his country's honour, as more than breaking a lance with the British bureaucracy, as, in fact, signing its death warrant, and at last fulfilling " our duty " to Indians. After seven years' trial the innocence of the spectator in 1926 has passed away with the knowledge that Mr. Montagu's lance lies broken in the Archæological Museum at Calcutta, and that the supposed death warrant has been replaced by reprieves satisfactory to the bureaucracy.

There is no possible doubt whatever that the reform schemes shook the " steel frame " at first, frightening Young England, who thought of adopting an Indian career, because it combined great power with unusual freedom, high pay, splendid pensions, and glittering prizes, and affecting adversely recruitment for the Indian services. But when Mr. Lloyd George in 1922 delivered his "steel frame" speech, in which he declared that he could see no period when India could dispense with British civil servants; and when Parliament in 1925 passed " The Government of India

(Civil Services)" Act to not only increase the emoluments of civil servants, but to remove their salaries from the control and vote of the Indian National Assembly; and last, but not least, when it became clear that the Indian Civil Service not only administered, but governed, India, in spite of the new reforms, just as it administered and governed India before the reforms, then Young England's confidence was restored, and recruitment went on merrily again.

What Indian Nationalists wanted and asked for was an Indian Executive responsible to an Indian parliament, with authority not only to appoint and dismiss its own servants, but, most of all, to initiate its own policy. None of these things have they got; instead, Indianisation of the Government and the Administration seems further off, because British rule is camouflaged by the forms of constitutional government. In consequence the winter of India's discontent deepens, and her distrust in British honour and British pledges mounts Himalaya-high.

Apologists for Great Britain dishonouring her promises and agreements point to the recent recommendations of the Lee Commission (1925) that in future the proportion of Indian recruitment to the Indian Civil Service and the Indian Service of Engineers will be 60 per cent., to the Indian Police 50 per cent., and to the Indian Forest Service 75 per cent. But the apologists neglect to state that, with rare exceptions, the superior posts, the best-paid appointments, are still reserved for Britons, and that Indians are excluded from administering their own country for no other reason than that they do not belong to the ruling race.

For this gross inequality of treatment and for this lamentable denial of justice, of partnership and co-operation, the same apologists trump up the excuse of "efficiency," pretending that Britons are more efficient than Indians. After the neglect of education of the masses; after the neglect of sanitation and medical services of the villages; after the neglect to keep law and order between Hindus and Muslims; after the neglect of housing of the poor; after the neglect to protect the peasants from the money-lenders by providing agricultural banks; after the comparative neglect to improve and develop agriculture; after the neglect to foster Indian industries; after the Back Bay scandal of Bombay, "with its wicked waste of money"; after the New Delhi scandal; after the exploitation of the great cities of Bombay, Calcutta, Madras, etc., by British profiteers, who have captured the tramways, electric lighting, and other public services; after the manipulation of Indian currency in the interests of London, the less said about British efficiency the better.

The efficiency in exploitation, in which Britons pre-eminently excel, is one of the chief causes of Indian poverty, and the sooner India is rid of British efficiency the sooner she will recover financially and morally.

Another feature of British government of India overlooked or carefully concealed by its apologists, who wish to continue it in defiance of a parliamentary promise to end it, is that it is the *costliest government in the world of the poorest country in the world*, and constitutes in this respect a permanent cause of impoverishment and unemployment. Though all Britons are not Shylocks, they have taken their pound of flesh out of Indians, for they have not forced their services on India for nothing, or for next to nothing, or on a modest scale, like the Burnham scale, or at a rate which Indians would fix for themselves and be thankful. The British did not consult Indians, did not appoint an Indian National Board of Wages, when they determined what salaries and what pensions and what perquisites Indians must pay them for their unsolicited attentions. Indians were not even asked for their advice as to the hours of labour, the length of service to qualify for pension, the annual holidays, or anything pertaining to the hiring of the gentlemen of England to do the work which Indians had formerly done, and which they very naturally desired to continue to do. Workmen who work for masters whose men are on strike are called "blacklegs." British Imperialists not only took the "jobs" from Indians in India, but fixed their own terms to their own satisfaction.

British bureaucrats, or their spokesmen, added insult to injury, for they told Indians whom they had displaced, with that deference and politeness which is so characteristic of Westerners, "It may be a historical fact that you have ruled your country for countless ages, that even after the Moghul conquest you continued to administer your country, that you were pioneers in civilisation when we were barbarians, but you have fallen behind in the race, especially in organisation, industrial and military, and you must pay the penalty of your backwardness in these all-important departments of life, and allow us to take the money out of your pockets and the bread out of your mouths, and to govern you not as you please, for, being your superiors, we know better than you what is good for you."

Here I make an appeal in all earnestness to Young England, and Scotland, and Wales. As Ireland has been under the heel of Great Britain, it should be unnecessary to appeal to Young Ireland. Be no party to the further exploitation of India and the deprivation of Indians of their natural right to govern and administer their own country. Remember that thousands of Indians are out of employment because of Britons occupying administrative and other posts which *by divine right* belong to Indians. Do unto others as you would that others should do unto you. Remember that these same Indians are well educated, many of them with University degrees, some of them claiming Cambridge and Oxford as their *alma mater.* Do not forget that Indians, in the fitness of things, are fitter to govern and administer their country than you are. If the contrary proposition was put to you that Indians or Germans could govern and administer Great Britain better than you, you would treat it with the derision it deserves. You would go a step further, and declare that, even if they could, that is no reason why they should, repeating Sir Henry Campbell-Bannerman's noble truth, "Good government is no substitute for self-government."

On that basis, because one race thought itself superior in the art of government to another, and by force of arms wrenched government from its hands, liberty would disappear from the earth, and slavery would become the established order. Banish, therefore, from your minds any idea of a career in India as unclean and unrighteous and unworthy. Refuse to be "blacklegs" of empire, and enrol yourselves under the flag of freedom, and fight for Indian self-government.

> "In the world's broad field of battle,
> In the bivouac of life,
> Be not like dumb driven cattle,
> Be a hero in the strife.

R. N. Cust, a retired Indian civil servant, said in his "Linguistic and Oriental Essays": "There is a constant drawing away of the wealth of India to England as Englishmen grow fat on accumulations made in India, while the Indian remains as lean as ever. . . . Every post of dignity and high emolument, civil and military, is held by a stranger and a foreigner. Akbar made fuller use of the subject races; we make none; it is the jealousy of the middle-class Briton, the hungry Scot, that wants his salary, that shuts out all native aspiration. . . . The consequences will be terrible." Mr. Cust knew what he was writing about, for his annual pension, which he drew from India, was equivalent to the income of several hundred poor Indians. Since Mr. Cust penned those words "we make none" a few posts of dignity and high emolument have been given to Indians, but for every post held by Englishmen it would be quite safe to say that five or ten Indians are well qualified to discharge the duties, and at less than half the cost.

As we have said before, the time has arrived for the Secretary of State for India to make it known throughout the United Kingdom that, in pursuance of the declaration made by Parliament in August, 1917, all public appointments in India in the future will be filled by an Indian executive, responsible to the Indian Legislature, and that Indians will be preferred to Englishmen.

Indianisation of the Army

Indianisation of the Army is urgently called for on two grounds: firstly, for the purpose of national defence, and secondly, for the purpose of national economy. The constant accusation of Indian Nationalists against the British Government of disarming and emasculating the people " with the deliberate intention of preventing their attainment of freedom and self-government " has never been refuted by British statesmen, and never can be. It is a historical fact that we have disarmed and emasculated the people, and that we have closed the Army as a career to Indian gentlemen up till the Great War; and everybody knows that that policy was pursued out of craven fear lest India fought her war of independence and turned the British, bag and baggage, out of India.

In the opinion of friends of freedom, and in the eyes of the world, this constitutes the greatest crime Great Britain has committed in India. How unpardonable this crime was, the world argues, appears when it is realised that Great Britain might have been defeated in the Great War, her army withdrawn from India, and India left without defence!

At last the truth has dawned dimly on the blurred imperial vision of England that India's imperative need is a national army, officered by Indians and controlled by the Indian Legislature. But how reluctantly and how ineffectually since the war was over, and the immediate danger past, has England gone to work to satisfy India's need. Justice does not seem to enter into the question, so low has England sunk in imperial obsession.

Towards a national army " ten vacancies have been reserved annually at Sandhurst for Indian cadets "; and in order to secure a suitable supply of recruits for these vacancies there has been established in India the Prince of Wales's Royal Indian Military College, at Dehra Dun, for a maximum of seventy boys to be in residence together. " The Government of India have recently made provision for the eventual complete Indianisation of eight units of the Indian Army." "Men have been promoted from the ranks to hold the Viceroy's commission." "It is only since the war that King's commissions have been granted to Indians." These are unvarnished excerpts from the official record "India in 1924-25." Able mathematicians have calculated from these data that the Indian Army may be "nationalised" in 800 years' time.

This procrastination, this fooling and trifling with India's needs and praiseworthy aspirations, is highly pleasing to the British bureaucracy in India, fighting for power and self-preservation, and to the Imperial party at home, but highly dishonourable and dangerous to England, lowering her in the scales of world-justice and intensifying the "demon of distrust and hatred" in India, which may lead to anarchy and chaos in that continent.

The good faith of Britain has not been improved by the Skeen Committee, recently appointed by the Government of India to inquire into the demand of the Indian Legislative Assembly for "an Indian Sandhurst." The Government of India actually accepted a resolution of the Assembly asking for the establishment of an Indian college for the training of commissioned officers in 1922, and then, after three years' delay, takes two steps to the rear by wasting more Indian time and more Indian money in a committee of inquiry.

Behold still another example of the "inefficiency" and "incompetency" of British officials to govern India in the interests of India, and, I must add, to govern India constitutionally, for when the paid officials shirk or shunt the policy laid down by the

Legislature the spirit of the Constitution is broken, and India is hurled back into unadulterated bureaucratic government, which Lord Balfour and other high-blown Tories denounce as anathema, an accursed thing.

In the press I have followed the cross-examinations and philandering of the Skeen Committee, and I attended one of its sittings in Delhi, and for *opera comique* I can commend it to my countrymen. But what may be comic opera to us is disgraceful buffoonery to India, and ought to be ended at once by Lord Birkenhead issuing instructions to the British officials in Delhi for whose folly he is responsible to get on with a Sandhurst for India without further delay.

On the financial side Indianisation of the Army will reduce the expenditure on the military octopus by anything from one-third to one-half, for Indian officers and Indian soldiers would consider themselves passing rich on half the pay required by British officers and British soldiers. Indianisation would further reduce the vast army of unemployed both in the middle and working classes.

Is it idle to ask British Imperialists to cease sneering at and taunting Indians on their non-fighting propensities or qualities after we have treated them like slaves for a hundred and fifty years, after we have thanked them for their bravery in the field and for helping us to win the Great War?

India is now united in her demand for a national army and self-government, however disunited she may be in religion, and the question I have to put to British Imperialists is, Are you not the greatest moral cowards in the world in obstructing the Indianisation of the Civil and Military Services and of the Government of India?

CHAPTER VIII

LABOUR AND TRADE UNIONS

TRADE unionism has a tremendous field of useful and glorious work before it in India in the emancipation of the masses from conditions which verge on economic slavery when they do not actually come within its borders. In no other country in the world is trade unionism more needful to fight the battle of the poor and submerged, who have not only been exposed, and are still exposed, to the merciless exploitation of capitalists, alien and indigenous, but have been taxed outrageously on their fields, their scanty produce, and the bare necessities of life, like salt, by a Government professing to be guided by the principles enunciated in the Sermon on the Mount.

Die-hards still exist in England and in India, men without a strain of humanity or mercy in their make-up, men who believe that God made the poor and not man, who denounce trade unions, would smash them, if they could, unmindful of the fact that these unions have been, and are, beneficial factors in the raising of the standard of life, in the increased contentment and well-being of the people, in the safety and security of the State, and in the prevention of revolution. But let the Die-hards read, mark, learn and inwardly digest what Lord Birkenhead, the high-priest of law and order, said when addressing the members of the Oxford University Conservative Association on May 22nd, 1926: "What were the legitimate claims of trade unions? They were entitled to be the trustees and guardians of the interests of those who had committed their affairs to their protection. It would indeed be an absurdity to suppose that in any trade dispute employers were always right and the men always wrong. The working classes of this country would not, in his judgment, have found themselves in the position which they rightly enjoyed to-day unless there had been great and powerful bodies able to assert, defend, and to make intelligible their claims."

The history of trade unionism in India practically dates from the termination of the Great War in 1918, when the rise in the cost of living, combined with capitalistic effort to reduce the miserably low wages still lower, drove the operatives into temporary or permanent unions in self-defence. The destitution of the people and their inability to pay contributions, the lack of education, the low standard of existence, the fact that a large proportion of the operatives are workers on the land by choice, and only temporary mill and mine workers by necessity when their labour is not required in the fields, the irregularity of time-keeping from aversion to the conditions, and the practice of bribery make the organisation of the trade unions exceedingly difficult. In spite of these difficulties, about 250,000 out of nearly two million workers under the Factories and Mines Act have enrolled themselves in trade unions; and the All India Trade Union Congress in 1926 contained fifty-two affiliated unions, with a total membership of over 125,000.

During disputes with employers the membership shoots up like spots in the sun, with a fine display of solidarity, sinking again immediately the storm is over, with little but a skeleton of an organisation left. The trade unions have gained some notable victories, especially when the mill hands of Bombay won the day in December, 1925, against the mill-owners, who tried to reduce their wages, when the Government of India were constrained to suspend—practically in perpetuity—the infamous excise duty on cotton goods.

The aims of the All India Trade Union Congress embrace (1) eight hours a day in factories and mines; (2) free and compulsory primary and technical education; (3) equality in Civil Service regulations, which at present favour "whites"; (4) abolition by law of the system of fines prevailing in industrial and commercial firms, railways, etc.; (5) establishment of labour bureaus; (6) national insurance against sickness, unemployment, and old age; (7) prohibition of employment of women underground in mines; (8) more women factory inspectors; (9) provision of *crèches* and day-nurseries in the vicinity of factories; (10) maternity benefits; (11) minimum wage; (12) improvement of the Workmen's Compensation Act; (13) a Trade Union Act on the lines of the British Act; (14) arbitration and conciliation legislation; (15) Labour representation in the central and provincial legislatures and in the Council of State; (16) a Labour party for India; (17) the removal of untouchability; (18) adult suffrage; (19) self-government for India and Indianisation of the public services; (20) affiliation and co-operation with the International Labour Movement, etc.

In the arena of social and moral improvement the trade union leaders support prohibition of drink, gambling, and other vices.

So far as representation in the legislatures is concerned, the Government of India and the Government of Great Britain have been most unequal and unfair in the treatment of Capital and Labour, as the following tables show:—

Employers' Representation in the Assembly

Province.	Number of Seats provided.			
	Europeans.	Landholders.	Indian Commerce.	Total Number of Seats.
1. Bengal . .	3	1	—	4
2. Bombay . .	2	—	1	3
3. Madras . .	1	1	1	3
4. Bihar and Orissa	—	1	—	1
5. United Provinces	1	1	—	2
6. The Punjab .	—	1	—	1
7. Central Provinces	—	1	—	1
8. Assam . .	1	—	—	1
9. Burma . .	1	—	—	1
Total .	9	6	2	17

Employers' Representation by Rotation in the Assembly

Province.	Constituencies.	Number of Seats by Rotation.
Bombay .	(1) Landholders in Sind . (2) Landholders in the Bombay Presidency except Sind .	1
Bombay .	(1) The Bombay Mill-owners' Association . . . (2) The Ahmedabad Mill-owners' Association . . .	1
Bengal .	(1) The Bengal National Chamber of Commerce . . (2) The Marwari Association . (3) The Bengal Mahajan Sabha.	1
	Total . . .	3

Employers' Representation in the Provincial Legislatures

Province.	Number of Seats provided.					
	Europeans.	Landholders.	Commerce and Industry.	Planting.	Mining.	Total Number of Seats.
1. Bengal	5	5	15	—	—	25
2. Bombay	2	3	7	—	—	12
3. Madras	1	6	5	1	—	13
4. Bihar and Orissa	1	5	—	1	2	9
5. United Provinces	1	6	3	—	—	10
6. The Punjab	—	4	2	—	—	6
7. Central Provinces	—	2	1	—	1	4
8 Assam	—	—	1	5	—	6
Total	10	31	34	7	3	85

Labour Representation in the Legislatures

Legislative Body.	Number of Seats provided by Nomination.	Remarks.
Central:		
1. Legislative Assembly.	1	It is not obligatory upon the Government of India to make this nomination.
Provincial:		
1. Assam	1	Nomination provided for by rules made under section 72A of the Government of India Act.
2. Bengal	2	
3. Bihar and Orissa.	1	
4. Bombay	1	
5. Burma	1	

It is a sad reflection on British ideals of fair play to think that Labour is represented by only one member in the Legislative Assembly, which is principally responsible for labour legislation in India, that he is a "nominee" of the Government, and that the Government can dispense with his nomination, as there is no *statutory* obligation to compel it to continue to nominate him in the future. Bravely as Mr. Joshi, the Labour member, has fought the good fight for the neglected and ignored workers, and bravely as he has been supported in the Assembly by such stalwarts as Lala Lajpat Rai, Dr. Datta, Mr. Goswami, Mr. Chaman Lall, Mr. Deoki Prasad Sinha, Mr. Acharya, and others, many of his measures for the amelioration of the miserable lot of the toilers of India have been squashed by the Government, hopelessly biassed and backed by a host of British officials and capitalists in India's mock Parliament.

The Trade Union Act (1926) legalises trade unions in India—under certain circumstances—which hitherto have existed on sufferance. With British Capitalism, supported by the Tory party, seeking to restrict the rights of British trade unionists, the need for co-operation between British and Indian Labour parties becomes more pronounced.

The All India Trade Union Congress protests against "special" constituencies and "nominations," and demands direct election, with adult suffrage. Pending the introduction of these democratic reforms, it asks for twelve seats for Labour against the twenty seats already given to Capital in the Central Legislature, and eighty seats for Labour against the eighty-five already granted to Capital in the Provincial Legislatures.

With regard to the need of linking up the All India Trade Union Congress with the British Labour Movement, as well as the International Labour Movement, in the interests of the workers of the world, to prevent the degradation of the standards of labour and of life by capitalists setting "sweated" against "un-sweated" labour, "coolie" conditions against more "civilised" conditions, I need add nothing to what I have already said in dealing with economic conditions. It remains for the British Trade Union Congress and the British Labour party to play the part of the good Samaritan and help its Indian brother out of the ditch in which the British bureaucracy has left it struggling for a hundred years or more.

The Independent Labour party has made the following suggestions: "Monetary assistance is important, but still more important is consultation and advice and training in methods of organisation. Special steps should be taken to enable the All India Trade Union Congress to affiliate to the International Federation of Trade Unions, to participate in its work, and to benefit by its knowledge and experience. Contact should be maintained between the headquarters of the Labour and Socialist International and those who are seeking to form a political Labour Movement, with a view to offering all possible assistance. The Internationals might consider the possibility of establishing a training college for the East, with its centre in India, with a view to equipping Indian and other Eastern workers for the duties of trade union and political development. Common action should be taken with the object of steadily raising the standards applied to Indian conditions under the regulations of the International Labour Office."

India is represented on the governing body of the International Labour Office.

Home Rule—Swaraj—which the writer maintains is the first and all-important and all-embracing step, the keystone to the arch of India's economic, industrial and political freedom, has also the active and whole-hearted support of the Independent Labour party, as we relate elsewhere, but which it is well to state here.

The General Strike in England in May, 1926, has many lessons for statesmen and working men in India as well as in other countries. For India the chief lesson seems to be the wisdom of nationalising its minerals, not only as an economic step against exploitation by private individuals, but also for the prevention of industrial warfare.

The mine-owners started the strike by locking out the miners because they refused to work longer hours and to accept a reduction in wages which meant starvation for them and their wives and children. On behalf of the miners the Transport and some other trade unions declared a sympathetic strike in order to present a solid phalanx against this assault of Capital upon the standard of life of their fellow-workmen. It is, therefore, fairly safe to say, "No private ownership of coal, no strike," for the nation would work the coal-mines for the benefit of the whole community, and not for the profit of a few. Of course strikes might possibly arise under nationalisation, but they would not be so likely, as the private and selfish interest would be removed.

Another lesson is that industrial warfare, like war, punishes the guilty and the innocent, the victims and the vanquished, the whole community, and that the vote, the political weapon, and parliamentary means (to which I have referred in another chapter), are the sanest and soundest for the attainment of industrial justice as well as political justice.

CHAPTER IX

EMIGRATION AND OVER-POPULATION

As a panacea for poverty and unemployment and over-population emigration has always stood high in the councils of Imperialists all over the world. British Imperialists have not lagged behind in this respect, preaching in season and out of season the necessity to "peg out claims for posterity," "to find places in the sun," to which the supposed surplus of population in Great Britain might emigrate, and there find full employment, and at remunerative rates. We need not stop to discuss here the fallacy of their gospel further than to state (1) that the small flow of emigration from Great Britain gives the lie to their argument, and (2) that statesmen in England have proclaimed and pressed the alternative of developing the home lands instead of appropriating other people's lands as the cure for British unemployment.

When it comes to a question of Indian unemployment, the British Imperialist finds himself on the horns of one or more dilemmas. His first dilemma, already stated, is that British Imperialists are a cause of unemployment in India, especially amongst the middle and professional classes, whose posts and means of livelihood they usurp, and that to propose emigration to members of these classes in order to administer British colonies would be unthinkable, impracticable, and insulting. His second dilemma bulges out in the awful fact that Indian labourers and traders are not welcomed in British colonies, except as serfs, as hewers of wood and drawers of water for Britons. In brief, British Imperialists demand a monopoly of power and position not only in India, but in the British Empire. Unable, therefore, to advocate their pet panacea for unemployment in India, they fall back on restriction of the population, and shovel out, without restriction, criticisms and censures on the Indian people for their prolificacy. In this they are again illogical, for in England they advocate prolificacy, the manufacture of innumerable "little Englanders," generated on imperial beer, to uphold the flag of Imperialism in India for ever.

Until British Imperialists resign their posts in India in favour of Indians out of employment, until Indians are allowed to exercise their own judgment in the government of their own country, until Indians have the opportunity of solving their unemployment problem by cultivating their own uncultivated lands, until Indians enjoy equal rights in all parts of the British Empire, all talk on the part of British Imperialists of either emigration or birth-control as remedies for unemployment is idle.

Against the assertion of British Imperialists that over-population is the root cause of India's poverty has to be set the complaint of Indian economists and Indian patriots that British rule, the most expensive in the world, and British exploitation of their country's resources, and British extravagance and waste on militarism, form the most formidable causes of India's impoverishment. But if the contention of British Imperialists with regard to over-population had any further foundation in truth, who so capable of interfering successfully, by education and legislation, with the customs of the people, in retarding the age and consummation of marriage as the natural check to growth in population, as Indians? For the sake of argument, let it be granted that over-population is a factor in the production of Indian poverty and unemployment; then it follows that a Government of foreigners, which fears to deal with the marriage laws and customs, ought to give place to a Government of Indians, which would have no fear in that respect. As a medical man, I am bound to point out the dangers of a social system which brings boys and girls together at early, if not immature, ages, and which encourages not only excessive breeding, but the breeding of defective children. Eugenics, the science of the production of healthy children, should command the attention of legislators more and more all over the world.

The conclusion that the disinterested and unprejudiced observer and investigator arrives at is, that British rule has not only failed to solve the awful problem of Indian poverty and unemployment, but has actually aggravated it.

Indians in the Empire

The grievances from which Indians suffer in the British Empire would fill a book, and my difficulty is to compress them into a chapter. At present there are about one and a half million Indians settled in different parts of the Empire, who may be divided into three classes: (1) unskilled labourers, either under indenture, as in the case of Fiji, Mauritius, Natal and the West Indies, or under some special system of recruitment, as in Ceylon and Malay States; (2) traders skilled artisans, clerks and professional men, who spontaneously have followed their countrymen (mentioned in the previous category) to serve their requirements; and (3) free immigrants, traders, labourers, under no indenture, etc., who have settled in the Dominions with the exception of South Africa, and in the East African colonies.

The chief grievances of India, as a member of the British Empire, are, firstly, that her nationals are definitely excluded by immigration laws from entering and permanently residing in some of the self-governing Dominions; secondly, that in those self-governing Dominions where her nationals have been admitted, in some cases actually invited, and allowed to reside for generations, they have been treated as "inferiors" and "serfs," denied the elementary rights of citizenship, the exercise of the vote, the holding of land, trading certificates, etc., and subjected to legislation of a discriminating, harsh and cruel character, having for its object their expulsion; and, thirdly, that in the Crown colonies and mandated territories, still under the control of the Colonial Office, her nationals have been refused equal rights with whites, and also political, economic and social justice.

At the Imperial Conference of 1921 the representatives from the Dominions, with the exception of the South African delegates, agreed "that in the interests of the solidarity of the British Commonwealth it was desirable that the rights of British Indians (lawfully domiciled in the Empire) to citizenship should be recognised." Subsequently a deputation from India visited Canada, New Zealand and Australia in order to directly negotiate with the respective Governments of these countries with a view to the removal of the disabilities from which resident Indians were suffering, but met with little or no success.

At the Imperial Conference of 1923 the 1921 resolution was indorsed by all the Dominions save South Africa, and a suggestion accepted that a Colonies Committee be appointed by the Government of India to confer with the Colonial Office regarding the status of British Indians domiciled in British colonies, protectorates and mandated territories, and with Committees of the Dominions, as to their status in the Dominions.

Kenya.—Mr. J. H. Thomas announced in the House of Commons on August 7th, 1924, the result of the conferences which he had had with the Colonies Committee in regard to Kenya, Fiji and Tanganyika. In spite of the fact that Kenya owes much to Indian labour and Indian capital for its development, and that Indians outnumber Europeans, Indians are debarred from holding agricultural lands in the highlands of the colony, and from adequate representation upon the Legislative Council, which is dominated by Britons, who form a minority of the community. These notable disabilities, with threats of compulsory segregation and of total prohibition of immigration from India, produced strong racial feeling and strained relations between the Indian and British settlers in the colony, which had their reverberations throughout India in vehement protests in the press, in public demonstrations, and in the Indian Legislature, so that the Government of India was constrained to make serious representations to the Colonial Office. When the British Colonial Office came down on the side of the British settlers in the White Paper of 1923, resentment in India reached such a pitch that a Bill to regulate the entry into, and residence in, British India of persons domiciled in other

British possessions, was introduced, considered and passed in one day by the Legislative Assembly as a protest.

Mr. Thomas, as Colonial Secretary, decided—(1) that an Ordinance which had been framed on the lines of restricting Indian immigration should not be enacted; (2) that Indians should select five members to be nominated by the Governor to the Legislative Council; (3) that there should be no change in policy regarding the franchise and the highlands, as it was proposed to set apart an area in the lowlands for agricultural immigrants from India.

In other colonies, like British Guiana, Trinidad, Jamaica, Ceylon and Mauritius, British Indians enjoy the same rights as other British citizens, without any discrimination on the ground of race.

Fiji.—In Fiji, however, Indians have serious grievances, and demand more adequate representation upon the Legislative Council, a municipal franchise based upon a common electoral roll, a minimum wage fixed in proportion to the cost of living, and the abolition of the poll-tax, which is not levied on the rest of the inhabitants.

Tanganyika.—In Tanganyika the grievances of Indians were so substantial that the Government of India protested to the Colonial Office, especially against three Ordinances introduced in 1923 imposing certain taxes and rates, requiring the yearly renewal of trade licences and the keeping of accounts in English, Swahili, or French, which were deemed discriminatory against Indian residents, and which led to strikes.

Indians in Rhodesia find themselves in the year of grace 1927 under the harrow, and this in spite of the fact that the British South Africa Company, of evil reputation, which usurped the territories belonging to the Matabeles, has been replaced by Crown Colony administration after the grant of responsible government. Indians are still required to hold "residential certificates" to permit them to continue to live in the colony, and these certificates, which Indians thought were available for all time, will now lapse in case of those who are absent from the colony for three years or more. Admitted on sufferance, Indians regard this new administrative regulation as a *device to hound them out of Rhodesia*, although they obtained a "concession" that "individual cases" would be considered by the principal immigration officer up till October 5th, 1926.

The burden of the white man's government in Rhodesia, as well as its bent, can be estimated by the reservation figures. A total of 76,230 square miles is reserved for Europeans, while the natives, who outnumber the Europeans by more than twenty to one, will have 45,280 square miles reserved to them.

Indians in South Africa

The history of British Indians in South Africa, extending over sixty-six years, is full of trouble for Indians, and reflects sadly upon the morality and sense of justice of both British and Dutch, who have exploited that portion of the world in their own selfish interests, unmindful of their duties to natives or to Indians. The worship of Mammon by white men has been the curse of South Africa, as it has been the curse of Morocco, Egypt, India, China, etc. The infidelity of the white man to the ideals and religion which he preaches, but rarely practises, is nowhere more pronounced than in South Africa.

In the early days of colonisation the white man

encouraged and welcomed the Indian immigrant, especially in Natal, whose agricultural success was won largely by his patience and industry in the sugar plantations. Recruitment in India prospered through promises contained in a Royal Proclamation, decreeing that no disability or limitation of legal rights would be imposed upon any one by reason of colour, race, or religion, and also through grants of land. At the same time Indian traders were encouraged to enter South Africa in order to cater for the needs of their fellow-countrymen.

When the gold mines were discovered many of these Indians, or their descendants, flocked into the South African Republic, in spite of the persecution to which they were compelled to submit, and which was used by British Imperialists as one of the arguments for waging war against Mr. Kruger's Government.

After the Boer War the British gradually hardened their hearts against the Indian settlers, and finally united with the Dutch in adopting an anti-Indian policy, on the plea that Indians were competing with whites in trade and agriculture. One has to acknowledge with surprise and regret that even the White South African Labour party has been drawn into the vortex of imperial grab, initiated by its quondam enemies the plutocrats, and, instead of incorporating Indians into its trade unions, has sanctioned and supported anti-Indian legislation with a view to establishing "a white South Africa on the basis of a depressed black South Africa."

Of the 155,000 Indians in South Africa about 135,000 dwell in Natal, 12,000 in the Transvaal, 8,000 in the Cape, and 600 in the Orange River Colony.

Disfranchised for parliamentary purposes by a provision in the Constitution of the Union of South Africa "excluding from the franchise natives of any country not at the time possessing elective institutions," this disability has not been removed from Indians since the Montagu-Chelmsford Reforms. In the Cape and Orange River Provinces Indians still enjoy the municipal franchise, but in 1925 the municipal franchise in Natal was taken from them. In 1919 a Commission appointed by the Union Government recommended the retention of a law prohibiting the ownership of land by Asiatics in the Transvaal, and the withdrawal of the right, which Indians had previously exercised, to purchase and own land in the uplands of Natal, but, as a result of the protest of the Government of India, this latter proposal of the Commission was not accepted by the Union Government. Anti-Indian legislation culminated in "the Areas Reservation and Immigration and Registration (Further Provision) Bill," introduced by General Hertzog's Government in the South African Union Parliament in 1926, the main provisions of which are—

1. The withdrawal of the right of Indians to buy or lease land anywhere in the Union, except within thirty miles of the Natal coast and within this area only from other Indians already in possession.
2. In townships the right of Indians to buy or lease property, or to be licensed for trade, shall be restricted to areas to be defined by the local municipality, upon which Indians have no representation.
3. Indians' licences to trade at present held outside the permitted areas may be withdrawn, the declared intention being to withdraw them.

This measure was described by the Minister who introduced it as "pressure," but Indians regard it as "oppression," to make their lives intolerable and to clear them out of South Africa. The indignation and resentment which it has caused in India is as intense as it is universal, and can best be estimated by the fact that it has united the Government of India with the legislatures of India and the people of India as they have never been united before in the demand for its withdrawal, or, if passed by the Government of South Africa, for its veto by the Imperial Parliament.

The Government of India considers it a question of international importance, and has despatched a deputation to South Africa to confer with General Hertzog's Government upon it. If this oppressive measure were enacted and enforced it might be the rock upon which the British Empire would split, for a self-governing and self-respecting India would refuse to form a part of a White Empire, and other "coloured nations" at present within the Empire would probably follow suit. It would be a deadly blow at the great ideal of converting the British Empire into a true Commonwealth of free nations, in which state, in the opinion of the writer, it alone can live and move and have its being.

In India this anti-Indian legislation is regarded as a breach of treaty solemnly entered into between the Governments of India and Natal, which was made before the South African Union was established, but which is binding upon the Union by section 148 of the South Africa Act, which declares that all rights and obligations which are binding on any of the colonies devolve upon the Union. Further, it appears to be a flagrant breach of the Smuts-Gandhi Agreement of 1914, by which India agreed to waive the right of entry of Indians as British citizens into South Africa on the condition that the rights of those already domiciled there should be respected. The Indians' Relief Act of 1914 embodied the terms of the Smuts-Gandhi settlement, and was enacted with the sanction of all South African political parties.

The citation of a speech by General Smuts at the Imperial Conference in 1917 may be helpful to an understanding of the problem :—

"In South Africa there has been this fundamental trouble, that the white community have been afraid to open the door too wide to Indian immigration. We are not a homogeneous population. We are a white population on a black continent, and the settlers in South Africa have for many years been actuated by the fear that to open the door to another non-white race would make the position of a few whites in South Africa very dangerous indeed. It is because of that fear that they have adopted an attitude which sometimes, I am bound to admit, has assumed the outward form, although not the reality, of intolerance. Luckily we have got over these difficulties. The visit of the late Mr. Gokhale to South Africa did an enormous amount of good. His visit was followed later by that of Sir Benjamin Robertson, a distinguished public servant of India, who also assisted the Government to overcome great difficulties on this point some years ago. The result has been the legislation to which both the white and the Indian community in South Africa agreed. There is still difference of opinion on administrative matters of detail, some of which are referred to in the memorandum which is before us, but I feel sure, and I have always felt sure, that once the white community in South Africa were rid of the fear that they were going to be flooded by unlimited immigration from India, other questions would be considered subsidiary and would become easily and perfectly soluble. This is the position in which we are now ; the fear which formerly obsessed the settlers there has been removed ; the great principle of restricting immigration, for which they have contended, is on our statute book with the consent of the Indian population in South Africa and the Indian authorities in India, and, that being so, I think that the door is open for the statesmanlike solution of all the minor administrative trouble which occurred, and will occur, from time to time. Of course the main improvement has been the calling of India to the Council Chamber of the Empire. Here, if any question proves difficult of treatment, we can discuss it in a friendly way and try to find in consultation a solution, and I am sure we shall ever find it. I, for one, do not consider that amongst the multitudinous problems which confront us in our country the question of India will trouble us much in the future."

The Government of India, in a despatch, also wrote as follows :—

" Fresh restrictions would be regarded, not only by the Indian community in South Africa, but also by the Government and people of India, as a breach of the settlement of 1914, which is universally accepted as a guarantee that the status which the Indian community has acquired in 1914 would at least be maintained. As has already been said, any understanding to administer laws in a just manner is meaningless if the rights which Indians are entitled to exercise under these laws could be restricted at will by fresh legislation."

As both India and South Africa are members on an equal footing of the British Imperial Conference, and also the League of Nations, submission of their differences to one or other of these bodies would be to their mutual interest and to the advantage of the comity of nations.

Personally I feel (1) that India sacrificed too much in the Smuts-Gandhi Agreement, and (2) that India will never pull her full weight for the benefit of her nationals in international or intercolonial agreements until she enjoys complete Dominion status.

Indians in Irak

The history of Indians in Irak (Mesopotamia) is one of the latest chapters in imperial dishonesty. To the cynic it is laughable, to the serious it is lamentable, and to the poor Indian, who was optimistic and hopeful to find in it a fair field and no favour for his future occupation and means of livelihood, it is lachrymatory.

The history of the Great War records, or will record, that Indians tumbled over each other to serve Great Britain; that among other exploits the Indian Expeditionary Force captured Irak from the Turks; that Indians lost more lives and money in Mesopotamia than in any other part of the world; that Indians, being simple and unsophisticated, and guided by the history of their own country, believed that the spoils of war went to the victors, and that in consequence Irak would fall to their lot. But they counted without their hosts, the conquerors of their own country. Honour! There may be among thieves, but none among Imperialists; at least, that was the experience of Indian Imperialists.

At first they were deceived and pleased, for immediately after the occupation of Irak a "steel-frame" administration, after the Anglo-Indian pattern, was fixed up in place of the Turkish *régime*, and manned almost entirely by Indians with a few British at the top. This glory did not last long, for the men of Irak protested that the war was for self-determination, that they were determined to govern themselves, and pushed their determination with stout hearts and strong arms, when the British and Indian Imperialists fell upon those patriots, fighting for their own country, and slaughtered them as the Germans did the Belgians.

This warlike patriotism on the part of the Irakians acted like magic on British Imperialists, who conceded to Irakian force, displayed in a few months' fighting, more self-government than they conceded to Indian reason, extending over a hundred years. Irak won a Parliament, a Cabinet, a King, Arabic as the official language, and the Indianised administration was converted in the twinkling of an eye into an Arabian administration. Thousands of Indians were packed out of Mesopotamia like herrings, and the hundreds, who were retained to teach Arabs, were axed as soon as the Arabs learnt their work.

The Anglo-Irak Treaty contains provisions for the employment of British officials on ten years' contracts at remunerative rates, but contains no satisfactory conditions for the few Indian officials still remaining in the service ; and by it Irak was transferred from the control of the India Office to that of the Colonial Office.

Among other lessons, the Mesopotamian adventure has taught Indians that they are good enough to pick chestnuts out of the fire for Britons, but not good enough to participate in eating them on terms of equality, and that physical force appeals more to British Imperialists than moral or intellectual force.

" It will be plain from this summary that the treatment accorded to Indian nationals in other parts of the British Empire is at present a very living issue in the eyes of educated Indian opinion. It is a matter upon which Indian intellectuals, without regard to political divisions or party aims, stand united. Anything which is regarded as an aspersion upon India's dignity is bitterly resented, and exercises a marked influence upon the course of domestic politics. The future as well as the immediate implications of the whole question are formidable. The course of relations not merely between India and the rest of the Empire, but between Asia and Europe, may well depend upon the ability of British statesmanship to convince the educated classes of India that there is room for them within the commonwealth to rise to the full height of their aspirations, and to attain the privileges and the responsibilities which the self-governing Dominions enjoy."

This is from the Official Record of the Government of India for 1924–25, to which the writer has only to add, as Indians suffer from political and other disabilities in India under direct British rule, can the Government of Great Britain expect them to escape from disabilities in the rest of the Empire? Great Britain must clean her own slate first by granting India full responsible government, and then the Dominions and Colonies will clean theirs.

CHAPTER X

PUBLIC HEALTH AND WAR AGAINST DISEASE

NEXT to education of the masses and defence against foreign invasion, most people would maintain that the duty of Government is to defend the people against the ravages of disease and drink, which are greater than the ravages of war. Lord Curzon, when Viceroy, seemed to place defence against disease first in his favourite quotation, "Salus populi suprema lex"—the health of the people is the supreme law.

I include drink with disease because alcoholism and drug-taking are such important factors in the production of disease, as well as of moral and material deterioration. Amongst racial poisons, producing physical, mental and moral degeneration in the stock, alcohol occupies the unenviable position of being second in the list, syphilis coming first. How far alcohol may lead to the contraction of syphilis may be a matter of conjecture, but the exciting and exacerbating action of alcohol on syphilis is well known to medical science. The relationship between alcoholism and tuberculosis, as cause and effect, has been demonstrated by international congresses on tuberculosis, when resolutions have been passed recommending that the fight against disease should be combined with the fight against alcoholism. Apart from these hydra-headed diseases, alcohol contributes indirectly to other ills to which flesh is heir by reducing the natural powers of resistance, and directly by causing fatty and fibrous diseases of the heart, kidneys, liver, alcoholic neuritis and paralysis, delirium tremens, alcoholic mania, etc. Lieut.-Colonel Sir Leonard Rogers, a distinguished physician, well known in India, points out the more deleterious effects of drink in hot climates like India. The saving in human lives through the decreased death-rate in the United States of America under Prohibition has been estimated at a million in the last five years.

Whether drink-caused disease is included or excluded, the function of Government consists in (1) prevention of disease and (2) provision for its proper treatment.

Under the first head would come the organisation of self-government in towns, villages, districts, provinces, and for all India, with complete control of, and responsibility for, public health and public morality ; sanitation, water supply, housing and town planning, roads, irrigation, drainage, etc., and under the second head provision of hospitals, medical colleges, sanatoria for tuberculosis, leprosy, etc., research laboratories, clinics, health insurance, etc., all under public control.

The charges and grievances of Indians against their British overlords regarding this question of public health are as grave as they are numerous.

The gravest charge is that public health matters have not been entrusted to Indians through representative institutions, through district boards, municipalities, provincial and central legislative councils, not even under the recent reforms, which nominally transferred these functions to Indians, but in reality reserved them to British officials, who, retaining control of the purse, have consistently and persistently starved this vital service, with fearful injury to the health and happiness of the people of India. Since the reform of the councils more money has been allotted to, and spent on, sanitation and on education, thanks to the pressure which Indians have been able to bring to bear on the bureaucracy. But until Indians control finance there is no hope for great schemes of sanitation, housing, etc., being carried out, and for great improvement in the public health.

Money can always be found by British officials for the Army, which is the basis of their power, or for increasing their own salaries and emoluments, but when it comes to finding money to benefit Indians by betterment in their homes and sanitary surroundings, then the alien taskmasters cry, "Halt!", and the bureaucratic economy axe comes down with a thud.

Let the official year-book "India in 1924–25" tell the tale: "Among the most pressing problems of India's public health is the infant mortality. It has been calculated that every year some two million Indian babies die. Birth registration is still too casual to afford precise data, but it may be stated with confidence that one in six, or perhaps even one in five, of the infants born in India perishes within the first year of life. In crowded and industrial cities the rate is even more lamentable, and it is believed that in certain localities the death-rate varies from over 200 to 600 per 1,000. In England the corresponding rate averages about 80 per 1,000. *Of late much attention has been directed to remedial measures.*"

The italics are mine because I want Lord Birkenhead and the British people to realise how we have been "unworthy trustees" of the babies of India. Mr. Winston Churchill, in his terminologically graphic way, might describe the Government of India as the "baby-killer of India," despatching them by millions, and too often painfully slowly.

The Official Recorder, after pointing out the lateness of the day, passes on to mention whose attention is being directed to remedial measures: "Lady Chelmsford initiated an All India Maternity and Infant Welfare League. Lady Reading has taken up the work, and has initiated the National Baby Week." The first observation that the reader or any disinterested person naturally makes is, "How kind of these ladies to take up the work of their husbands, the Viceroys of India, and of the Secretary of State for India!" The second observation would follow in a totally different vein, namely, "the most pressing problem of India's public health" cannot be adequately dealt with by voluntary associations, even when patronised by the wives of the most eminent officials and by members who display the keenest enthusiasm. Thirdly, this most pressing problem cannot honourably or in justice to India's dying millions be shirked by the Government of India and the Government of Britain by relegating it to eleemosynary aid and voluntary associations. Lastly, "remedial measures" mean an Indianised medical and nursing service, national health insurance, maternity benefit, regulations *re* female labour, minimum wages, slum clearage, housing and town planning schemes, with provision of open spaces and playing grounds for young and old, sanitation on modern lines, etc., with the necessary legislation, provincial, municipal and central.

The sooner Lord Birkenhead gets on with these "remedial measures," involving revision of the Constitution and the granting of responsible government at once, and not in 1929, or gets out, the better for Indian babies and India's health.

Another quotation from the Official Recorder ought to be helpful. It is the following: "Of immediate bearing on the progress of sanitation in India is the advance of medical research in India. In this field financial stringency has of late hampered development, but in the Budget for 1925–26 provision has been made once more for a subvention to the Indian Research Fund Association, whose activities have suffered temporarily from retrenchment."

The full value of this statement as to the relationship between sanitation and research may be gleaned when vital statistics are studied, and when the heavy toll every year of preventable diseases like cholera, plague, malaria, smallpox, and tuberculosis is set forth.

The Statistical Abstract for British India gives the following death-roll :—

Year.	Population in Millions.	Cholera.	Small-pox.	Plague.	Fevers.	Respiratory.
1914	238½	280,730	76,590	260,474	4,000,000	261,000
1918	238	560,803	93,000	440,752	11,000,000	431,000
1923	241½	73,000	44,000	229,649	3,700,000	297,000

From the same abstract we learn the death-rate per thousand, viz. :—

	1914.	1918.	1919.	1923.
	30	62·46	35·81	25
In towns . . .	33·21	56·76	38·51	29·27
In rural districts .	29·71	62·98	35·63	24·58

The average length of life in India is 23·5 years, in Japan 44·5 and in England 53·5.

A careful study of these figures should make Lord Birkenhead pause before he again claims that his countrymen are not, and have not been, " unworthy trustees " of India's suffering millions. A personal inspection by his lordship of some of the towns and villages of British India would reveal such an appalling condition of housing and absence of general sanitation that he would stand aghast and never breathe the word " trusteeship " again. In the one-room tenements of Bombay, "the glorious gate of the East," he would understand why 828 out of every thousand babies born died within a year in 1922. In the mud and straw hovels of the villages, with low roofs and no windows, with no loophole for light and air to enter unless the door was open, or unless, fortunately, wear and tear had produced peepholes in the roof the better to see the stars by, with a ben for any cattle and a nook for the family, he would comprehend why, in spite of the sun and the salubrious climate, tuberculosis and epidemic diseases decimated the peasants, and ran their death-rate a close shave with that of dwellers in the towns. When his lordship's keen eye met the stagnant pool near by, and saw the mosquito flourishing on the surface of the waters undisturbed by kerosene, malaria, with all its terrors, would give him haunting fears by day as well as by night. When he learnt that the same pool or reservoir on occasion did duty for drinking water, as well as for ablution of the body and clothes, cholera and dysentery would rise before his vision, with all their horrors. When, further, his lordship discovered in the vast majority of villages neither dispensary, nor doctor, nor nurse, he would cry, " God help the people." When, finally, he found frantic poverty lurking at the door of the villagers, who rarely partake of one square meal per day, and consequently lack the stamina to resist disease, his lordship would give up the ghost. Then where would merrie England be, without its merrie lord and his merrie speeches on "the glittering prizes won by the sword"?

In one of his many brilliant oratorical efforts Lord Curzon spoke of "the real people of India" in the following terms: "It is the Indian poor, the Indian peasant, the patient, humble, silent millions, the 80 per cent. who subsist by agriculture, who know very little of politics, but who profit or suffer by their results, and whom men's eyes, even the eyes of their own countrymen, too often forget, to whom I refer. He has been in the background of every policy for which I have been responsible, of every surplus of which I have assisted in the disposition. We see him not in the splendour and opulence, nor even in the squalor, of great cities; he reads no newspapers, for, as a rule, he cannot read at all; he has no politics. But he is the bone and sinew of the country; by the sweat of his brow the soil is tilled; from his labour comes one-fourth of the national income. *He should be the first and the final object of every Viceroy's regard.*"

With my own eyes I have seen the peasants in every village which I have inspected living in overcrowded hovels, which would be more accurately described as kennels, in surroundings of dirt, discomfort, and squalor, indicative of the palæolithic period, and for the most part without a schoolmaster, a doctor, or nurse. I have, therefore, been forced to the conclusion that so far as education, sanitation, and medical care

are concerned, the peasant has been the last and forgotten object of every Viceroy's regard.

In the same oration Lord Curzon boasted that " it is for the peasant in the main that we have twice reduced the salt tax." Lord Curzon ought to have known that a Government which puts any tax on the salt of the poor is a cruel monster, sapping the vitality of the people and spreading foul diseases which arise from deficiencies of salt in their daily food.

In 1923–24 the revenue from salt amounted to 10,01,50,870 rupees, which Lord Curzon's successors will try to defend by saying that, as the tax is spread over so many millions of people, it cannot be provocative of much harm, forgetting, firstly, that no Government in England which imposed a tax on salt could live for a single week, and, secondly, that Governments, especially alien Governments, have no moral right to tax an essential food of the people.

This chronic crime of the British authorities in India becomes greater when the debasing and degenerating influences of opium and alcohol, which are also fostered by the Government, are taken into consideration.

I should like to conduct Lord Birkenhead, or any future Secretary of State for India, not only to the villages, but to the imperial city of Delhi, where he would view imperial trusteeship in all its glory. For choice I should take him first to a bit of Old Delhi, not to the ancient gates; not to the Fort, with its marble palaces and its chamber, with its scales of justice, loaded heavily by the imaginative Imperialist so that they always tip in favour of the West; not to the Ridge, where a monument towers to the memory of the British victims of British Imperialism, mentioning them by name, without any corresponding monument or tablet with the names of the Indian patriots who died in defence of their country against the British invader; not to the marvellous Mosque, where he might pray for forgiveness not only for past sins, but for sins which he was going to commit, for Imperialists live in perpetual sin; to these places of artistic and historic interest Cook's guide would go first; but, being a doctor most interested in humanity, I should lead him straightway to the homes of the poor, who have long been the special subjects or slaves of British solicitude and British conceptions of sanitation. There the picture of dirt and disorder, of wretched hovels and indescribable horrors, without drainage, sanitation, or adequate scavengering, with human excrements in every narrow alley, filling the air with foul stenches worse than any Stygian pool, a beautiful breeding ground for pestilence and disease, of groups of men and women and children sitting on cleared ground away from their inhospitable huts, rudely huddled together, which were used as crowded shelters at night, of children emaciated from malnutrition, and men and women looking old and haggard long before their time, demands a Dante to depict.

Then Lord Birkenhead, with perfumed handkerchief to nostril glued, would implore me to lead him away to Modern Delhi, where the grass grows and the perfume of flowers pervades the air, where the British reside beyond the city walls in detached villas, fitted with every modern sanitary convenience to make life comfortable and disease rare, lighted by electricity, with pretty rose gardens and lawns neatly clipped, with the English Club close by, a large and handsome building, with spacious rooms, luxuriously furnished for billiards, bridge, smoking, eating, drinking and dancing, and situated in lovely grounds, amply provided for tennis and other outdoor games, with well-made and well-kept roads, and, best of all, with magnificent parks, where lofty trees and many-coloured flowers lend enchantment to the view, and make life worth living.

The Government buildings form a most pleasing picture to the eye, being well set back from the main road in spacious grounds, with beautiful beds of flowers and green lawns and graceful gravel walks. The centre of the buildings, which are all white and arranged in a half-moon, is occupied by the Parliament House, with the Administrative Offices forming the wings. Pleased with the outside, his lordship would express his pleasure with the internal aspect also of the National Assembly and with its acoustic properties, which he would test by eloquently reciting Scott's famous lines—

> "Breathes there the man, with soul so dead,
> Who never to himself hath said,
> 'This is my own, my native, land,'
> Whose heart hath ne'er within him burned
> As home his footsteps he has turned
> From wandering on a foreign strand?
>
> "If such there breathe, go, mark him well;
> For him no minstrel raptures swell,
> High though his titles, proud his name,
> Boundless his wealth as wish can claim;
> Despite these titles, power and pelf,
> The wretch concentred all in self,
> Living, shall forfeit fair renown,
> And, doubly dying, shall go down
> To the vile dust, from whence he sprung,
> Unwept, unhonoured, and unsung."

My imagination figured Lord Birkenhead, under the spell of poetic emotion and appreciation of patriotism in others, saying: "By God! standing in this Chamber, nominally consecrated to Indian liberty and Indian self-government, I understand the point of view of the Indian patriot. But tell me," he added in cooler and more critical vein, "what's wrong with this charming Chamber, and excellent block of Administrative Offices, and magnificent Government House, which the Viceroy occupies for one or two months in the year, and which must have cost a lot of money to build, that they should all be scrapped after a few years' use and a new Delhi created?"

"An imperial bee in the bonnet of Lord Hardinge and his bureaucratic advisers, I suppose, for Indians opposed it tooth-and-nail on the score of extravagance and inconvenience."

"Umph!" was the single word which escaped his lordship's lips.

A Government Rolls-Royce then bore us swiftly to Raisina, as New Delhi is called, situated some five or six miles away. Carefully avoiding Old Delhi—for his lordship was still suffering from nostalgia or some other nostril affection—we soon came upon brand-new roads, with embryonic trees springing up on either side, protected by casing from wind and weather and showing no signs of infantile mortality. "What glorious Hobbema Avenues these will become in the course of a few years!" ejaculated his lordship; "and those long rows of pretty white villas, with gardens already bedecked with flowers, what are they?"

"More residences for British officials," I replied.

"And these grand palaces dotted about?" queried his lordship.

"They are the extravagances to which the princes of India have been put by Government, and which they will occupy for a month or two in the year when the Chamber of Princes meets."

" And that pompous structure in the distance ? "

" That's the Viceregal Lodge."

" 'Lodge,' do you call it ? " his lordship mockingly repeated. " 'Emperor's palace,' say I." And then he inquired, " How many of these 'Lodges' in India may there be ? "

" Your lordship should ask the Viceroy," came my reply. " But of course, if Mahatma Gandhi were Viceroy—and to my mind he is the best man fitted to discharge the onerous duties of that exalted dignitary—he would stop all this imperial display and wild waste of India's restricted resources. In fact, he would prove the greatest benefactor India had ever had, for, living himself in simplicity, he would teach both British Imperialists and Indian princes how to live simply and honestly without bleeding the people of India white," I added.

" Ah," quickly responded Lord Birkenhead, dropping his native cynicism, " you may be right, and it may come to that. But what are those tall, gaunt, grim and ugly blocks over there ? "

When informed that they were " the new Imperial Administrative Offices," his lordship sadly remarked : " What a miserable contrast to those picturesque ones which we have just visited ! "

Pointing to a vast pile of modern architecture approaching completion and having the mixed appearance of a Roman amphitheatre and a Greek temple, where gods and goddesses might worship together according to the rites of Venus, his lordship quizzingly questioned, " What is that White Elephant ? "

On learning that it was the future battle-ground of

Indian Amphictyons, fighting for the moral and material progress of India, the future home of the Indian imitations of the House of Lords and House of Commons, the noble lord heatedly observed: "This gives the answer to my statement in the House of Lords, namely, 'To talk of India as an entity is as absurd as to talk of Europe as an entity,' for the British Viceroy and the British Executive Council and the British bureaucracy would never have erected these colossal structures and this new imperial city unless they believed that India is an 'entity'; they have branded me as one of the biggest fools in the world, and vengeance demands that I should take all power out of their hands by making these mock parliaments stern and stable realities."

Overlooking his lordship's spirit of vengeance in the circumstances, I could not resist exclaiming, "Bravo! bravissimo! Behold a Daniel come to judgment!"

On our return journey to Maiden's Hotel, where his lordship was staying incognito to avoid all pomp and revelry, which he loathes, and after allowing due time for cooling down, I made bold to ask his lordship, when passing under a sort of "Triumphal Arch," what impressions Old and New Delhi had left on his mind. Lord Birkenhead broke out in his happiest vein, so reminiscent of Oxonian fastidiousness and exhilaration, "Old Delhi's hell, modern Delhi's Paradise Lost, New Delhi's Paradise Regained, and I'm disappointed with my countrymen who are responsible for the lot."

In order to pour a little oil on the troubled waters I said, "Yes, I suppose our responsibility for all must be acknowledged, for the British Commissioner has bossed the municipality of Delhi since its inception, if he has not actually usurped all authority all along."

"And what is the estimated cost of New Delhi?" pursued his lordship.

"More than ten millions sterling when finished."

"Worse than Singapore," mused his lordship aloud. "The price of Imperialism never ceases to increase the burdens of Indian and British taxpayers, burdens which prevent them making adequate expenditure on education and sanitation, as we observed before. What blind and bankrupt statesmanship!"

Refreshed by sleep, the Secretary of State returned next morning to the subject of public health by asking for an explanation of the shortage of hospitals, research laboratories, sanatoria for leprosy and tuberculosis, dispensaries, doctors, nurses, etc.

In addition to the explanations already given, namely, (1) official fear to trust these things to Indians with complete financial and legislative and administrative control, (2) the *laissez-faire* policy of the Government to leave their provision to private and charitable organisations, and (3) the starvation of these vital services, there are (4) the practical monopolisation of the higher branches of the medical services by Britons and (5) the economic conditions of the villages, which cannot support doctors, nurses and dispensaries because they are too poor.

The first three explanations account for the extraordinary fact that only two or three sanatoria for leprosy and tuberculosis exist in the whole of British India, where these afflictions flourish, and for which sanatorial treatment and segregation are needed, especially for the prevention of their dissemination amongst the people. Under this head the British authorities in India deserve to be indicted for criminal neglect.

The Statistical Abstract for British India classifies hospitals as follows :—

NUMBER OF HOSPITALS FOR 1923

Class I.	Class III.	Class IV.	Class II.	Class V.	Class VI.
State Public.	Local Funds.	Private aided.	State Special, Police, Forests, Canals.	Private non-aided.	Railways.
418	2,952	281	473	783	424

TOTAL NUMBER OF BEDS FOR 1923

Classes I., III., IV., open to the public .	43,635
Classes II., V., VI., private and special .	13,938
Total	57,573

Regarding this grand total of 57,573 hospital beds for British India, exclusive of Indian States, with a population of 241 millions, it is up to the Government of India to explain why it has fallen so short as custodian of the medical and surgical treatment of the poor.

The total number of registered medical practitioners in Bengal in 1925 was a little over 4,600. The total population of the Province was about 46 millions. Therefore there is one practitioner to every 10,000 persons. If rural areas are taken only there is hardly one practitioner to 100,000 persons. This unsatisfactory supply of doctors in Bengal is repeated more or less in the other Provinces.

This brings us to the problem of medical and surgical aid in the villages, a problem which the Government of India never seems to have tackled and which urgently calls for solution. I visited villages within ten or twenty miles of Madras, Delhi and Lahore, where the poverty was so intense that when I asked the inhabitants why they did not convey serious cases of disease especially requiring surgical interference to save life in bullock-carts to the hospitals in the neighbouring cities, they replied, " The hire of a bullock-cart would cost two or three rupees (3*s.* to 6*s.*), and we haven't got the money." " What happens then ? " I inquired, when my informants laconically replied, " Oh, they miserably and sometimes painfully die, hoping for better things in a life beyond the grave." In other words, thousands, nay, tens of thousands, of villagers are allowed to die in agony every year by a paternal (?) Government, which talks about " trusteeship," without moving a finger or spending a penny to save them.

" My sapient tutors in the Indian Office never divulged this deplorable state of affairs in the villages," groaned the Secretary of State for India, evidently deeply stirred. " Now unfold to me your plan of campaign to meet this difficulty, for I should like to do something for these poor people before I leave office," continued his lordship.

" I have discussed this problem with many Indian doctors," I responded to his lordship's invitation, " and they all practically agree with me in principle that the solution lies with the Government in the creation of a State medical service, embracing both towns and villages, by means of which doctors, nurses, dispensaries, hospitals, sanatoria, research laboratories, etc., would be brought within reasonable reach of every one."

This service would differ from that provided under the Health Insurance Act in Great Britain in many important respects. For instance, everybody would be on the "panel," whether they availed themselves of the service or not; doctors, nurses, dispensers, etc., would be full-time salaried servants of the State; the scheme being non-contributory—for the vast majority of Indians are too poor to indulge in such a luxury—the whole cost would fall on the taxpayers; and the management, administration and control would be in the hands of the local authorities, village panchyats (to be re-created), district boards, municipalities, etc. Doctors and nurses would be appointed to groups of villages, and provided with the transport (motor ambulances, etc.) for getting from one to the other.

"That sounds all right," observed Lord Birkenhead, "but, critically examined, I see several objections to the plan. Firstly, it is unadulterated Socialism."

"Yes," I acknowledged, "but so is the postal and telegraph service, and also the Army and the railways, and many of the railways have been built and conducted at great cost for strategical purposes against possible foreign invaders. Surely your lordship won't raise the bogey of Socialism against a scheme to fight the invader within the gate, who is always active, namely, disease. Besides, the Indian medical service already in existence is unadulterated Socialism in the interests of the Europeans. Your lordship, therefore, cannot honestly object to Socialism in the interests of Indians."

"Granted!" smiled the Secretary of State; "but,

secondly, on a non-contributory basis the cost of this beautiful piece of Socialism would be prohibitive," he added.

"Not prohibitive," I answered, "because the same objection would apply to the army, which is non-productive, whereas a medical service would be productive, increasing the health as well as the wealth of the community, and the increased wealth would go a long way, if not all the way, to meeting the increased payment. Also Indianisation of the army and Indianisation of the medical service would reduce the expenditure of these services so enormously that the taxpayer might not be called upon to pay an extra pie. Lastly, if your lordship is still alarmed at the financial difficulties, you could commence by applying the scheme to the rural areas," to which his lordship nodded assent.

The noble lord then referred to the contention of Indians that the higher branches of the medical services were monopolised by Englishmen, and that in consequence gross injustice was inflicted upon the Indian people in general and upon Indian doctors in particular, and asked for information.

Put as briefly as possible, Provinces are divided into districts, each district covering fifty to 100 square miles, in each of which a civil surgeon is placed in charge, with responsibility for the sanitation, hospitals, dispensaries, vaccination, infectious diseases, births, deaths, etc., and with assistant surgeons and sub-assistant surgeons under him. The civil surgeons and assistant surgeons hold qualifications, which are registrable in Great Britain and India, while the sub-assistant surgeons may be described as a cheap class of doctors, who have only been trained for four years and whose qualifications are not recognised outside India. When a

Province like the Punjab is divided into ten districts, eight of the civil surgeoncies go to members of the Indian medical service, who are almost all Britons, one to an Indian, who has probably served about twenty years as assistant surgeon, and one to a Eurasian (Anglo-Indian) or Christian from the Indian Medical Department. Civil surgeons (almost all Englishmen) receive 1,250 to 2,500 rupees per month, with extras for travelling, lectureships, gaol appointments, etc., while assistant surgeons (all Indians) receive 225 to 450 rupees per month, and when promoted to civil surgeons from 600 to 1,000, and sub-assistant surgeons (Indians or Eurasians) 60 to 225 rupees per month.

Extraordinary anomalies arise from the rule that every district shall be provided with an English doctor, who is reserved from the Indian medical service of the army for the benefit of English families living in the district, even when these families only number four or five. At the same time this rule raises the vicious "colour bar" against Indian doctors, who are as well qualified and as capable as their English colleagues. If English people opt to live in India either as officials or non-officials, they have no right to inflict injustice on Indians by demanding medical attention at the expense of India or by maintaining the pernicious "colour bar."

So far as the public hospitals and medical colleges are concerned, there is not a vestige of popular government in administration, their government in most Provinces resting in the hands of the civil surgeon locally and of the inspector-general (or surgeon-general) of civil hospitals centrally, who are Englishmen with one exception. How disastrous to the patients and medical students and public health of India this concentration of autocratic powers in one or two officers is may be conceived when it is realised that they appoint all members of the staff to these important institutions.

Autocracy and abuse of power go together: autocracy, favouritism and nepotism are bedfellows. Men are too often appointed as physicians, and surgeons, and specialists, and professors who are entirely unfitted for their duties, with incalculable injury to patients and students alike. For instance, men are posted to special departments, like the eye or ear, who have never specialised on those delicate organs before. Further, men are jockeyed from physician to surgeon, and then to ophthalmologist or gynæcologist, on the exigencies of the occasion or on the whim of the Inspector-General. Sometimes they play at family post, and one man in his time fills many posts. The lowest degradation of a noble profession is reached when the doctor is converted into a jack-of-all-trades, filling several posts at the same time.

In Bengal this autocracy is checked to some degree by the fact that the Medical Faculty of the University of Calcutta contains a good proportion of Indian medical practitioners.

This system, or want of system, spells inefficiency in almost the whole medical service of India. Indians justifiably complain (1) that the Indian medical service is not recruited by the best English doctors, but by second-class men; (2) that these men practise in the Army for several years before being "lent" or "transferred" to Civil Service, and that Army practice frequently tends to rust and deterioration; (3) that the Medical Research and Medical Teaching Departments suffer from anæmia, with a surfeit of second-hand and second-rate Englishmen; (4) that medical students are deprived of a good scientific training, which is so essential and fundamental to excellence, and that psychologically they are adversely affected by sitting at the feet of undistinguished and unworthy professors, for whom they can have no respect, and who chop and change from anatomy to physiology, from medicine to surgery, from pharmacy to midwifery, with every passing breeze ; and (5) that *colour bar* rides rampant and triumphant throughout the medical service, Englishmen being appointed to the highest and best-paid posts, for which Indians, by their professional attainments and qualifications and experience, are better fitted, the minor posts being given to Indians.

Since the passing of the reforms in 1919 the Medical and Sanitary services have been transferred to the Minister of Education, who has power to appoint the staffs of hospitals and medical colleges, but if he dared to override the decision or recommendation of the Surgeon-General, and appointed Indians instead of Englishmen, he would be thrown out by the British officials who chose him, and a pliable Indian puppet put in his place. Outwardly British bureaucrats may appear to be as harmless as doves, but inwardly they are as wise as serpents when it comes to a question of power or a fight between Englishmen and Indians for lucrative posts.

In England independence and strength are esteemed as praiseworthy characteristics, but in India, when portrayed by Indians, they are counted as dangerous, and treated as dangerous, by British officials, who prefer and promote pliancy and subserviency.

When I drew the attention of the Inspector-General of Hospitals in a personal interview to the fact that only two or three Indians filled professional chairs in the University and Medical College at Lahore, he majestically remarked, " I consider that a good share."

In recent years some of the more glaring inconsistencies enumerated above with regard to chopping and changing and amalgamating of professorships have been modified, but not removed, in some medical colleges.

Before the war the percentage of Indians permitted in the Indian medical service was limited to 6, which was raised after the war, with 33⅓ as a maximum.

The whole Indian medical profession is up in arms against this intolerable state of affairs, which forms no negligible factor in Indian unrest.

On this recital Lord Birkenhead shook his head in dismay, and said, " This is not playing the game as we play it in England; this is un-English. What is necessary to cleanse these Augean stables and to remove these outstanding grievances of Indians?"

" Your question would be best answered by an Indian Medical Council composed of Indians, but, unfortunately, none is in existence, thanks to the policy of the British bureaucracy, which would deem such a body as undesirable, if not seditious. In the absence of such a council, I might suggest the following reforms, which have been formulated at one time or another by Indians, both privately and publicly :—

" (i.) The transference of public hospitals and medical colleges to democratically constituted governing bodies. Some advocate municipalisation.

" With regard to the creation of an Indian Medical Council, and on what lines, public opinion would be best consulted through the Legislative Assembly for All India. Indian doctors have given me to understand that such an institution is desirable, but that it should differ from the General Medical Council for Great Britain in that its authority should not be absolute, and that it should be amenable to the Courts of Justice through the Privy Council, but free from the Executive Government of India.

"(ii.) Indianisation of the Indian medical service, which is bound to come sooner or later. In view of this, your lordship would be well advised to put up notices in every university and hospital in Great Britain to the effect that British doctors in the future would have to seek appointments in India through Indian governing bodies, which would probably only select a small number who had reached great eminence in the profession as specialists or teachers. This would not preclude English doctors from practising privately in India.

"(iii.) The abolition of sub-assistant surgeons in the future as inadequately qualified men. This, of course, would not apply to existing sub-assistant surgeons.

"(iv.) Private hospitals, sanatoria, etc., must satisfy the Indian Medical Council or public authority of their fitness."

"These suggestions deserve, and shall have, my earnest consideration," said the Secretary of State, who showed the imponderable symptoms which attack a climber unaccustomed to the high altitudes of Mount Everest.

CHAPTER XI

PUBLIC HEALTH AND PROHIBITION

FROM the close relationship between alcoholism and disease, a relationship which may be accurately defined as cause and effect, as already pointed out in the beginning of the previous chapter, we approach prohibition and suppression of the liquor traffic as a great question of public health and national life.

In other places it is rightly and reasonably considered also as a great question of public morals and of law and order, for as a cause of immorality, disorder, and crime alcohol is unrivalled by any single agency. How many brothels, how many law-courts, how many prisons, might be closed if the manufacture and sale of intoxicating beverages were prohibited, I leave the Commissioner of Police and the Judges to honestly relate.

Here we confine ourselves to the health aspect of this enemy of the race, to this C3 population-producer, to the manufacturer of " little Indians " and " little Englanders " and " little Anglo-Indians," to this baby-killer, to this hospital and asylum filler, to this joy-killer, to this agent which steals away the brains, as Shakespeare said, and incapacitates man mentally as well as physically from rendering his best quota to the national service, the national health, and the national wealth.

In considering the health aspect we cannot, however, neglect the economic, for the two are wrapped together in the same winding sheet on the same funeral pyre. Low wages and poverty lead directly and indirectly to disease from underfeeding, insanitary housing, etc., to diseases, especially of malnutrition, like rickets, and to susceptibility to invading germs from reduced vitality. Expenditure on drink, especially in India, where wages are so scandalously low and poverty is so stupendously great and widespread, by reducing the earning capacity of the wage-earners and by intensifying the poverty of the poor, dooms the people to innumerable and avoidable diseases as well as to under-consumption, under-production, with agricultural and industrial depression and national poverty.

The manufacture and sale of intoxicants are, therefore, a curse to India, and the statesmen or the Government that fail to suppress them are "unworthy trustees" of India.

"I agree with you," intervened Lord Birkenhead *in an imaginary conversation*, "that 'gigantic evils' are associated with this traffic, but I wholly disagree with you in regard to Prohibition as a remedy. I frankly confess," continued his lordship, "that I have always championed the brewers and distillers and liquor-sellers at home, and consistency compels me to champion them in India. Besides, immediate introduction of Prohibition is 'unthinkable,' as Sir Basil Blackett, the Finance Member, said in the Indian Legislative Assembly in 1925, for it would cut off too big a slice of revenue, and lead to 'illicit distillation,' 'difficulties of enforcement,' and 'disrespect for the law,' and, he might have added, umbrage on the part of British residents in India, whose addiction to drink is so proverbial."

"Great statesmen," I replied, "are not the slaves,

but the subduers and overcomers, of difficulties. Prohibition in America, the greatest social experiment of modern times, has met with the difficulties and drawbacks which your lordship mentions, but American statesmen and the American people, instead of bending the knee to Baal and to the lawless elements in their country, are steadily and successfully removing the difficulties by perfecting the machinery of Prohibition. The social and economic gains from the adoption of Prohibition, the lowering of the death-rate from alcoholic diseases, the great reduction in crime, drunkenness and the consumption of liquor, the increased savings of the people, the improvement in industrial fitness and business conditions, stand out so conspicuously that America is keeping her waggon hitched to the star of Prohibition, in spite of all the froth, fury and propaganda of a prejudiced press and those financially interested in this traffic, which is so subversive of national health and national well-being."

The noble lord, parodying a bishop who went off the lines, retorted, " I would sooner see India free than sober."

" Precisely," came my response, " for when India is free she will take steps to ensure that she will be sober as well." India is ripe for Prohibition, and her great religions being so strongly opposed to drink should make the difficulties of successful enforcement much simpler and easier than in America.

Besides, the liquor trade in India is neither so well organised nor so powerful as in Europe or America, and already the Indian States of Bhopal, Bhavnagar, Palitana and Kathiawar have adopted prohibition of country-made liquors, while Travancore and Pudukottah have declared for Local Option.

The financial difficulty has been increased in recent years by the policy of the Government of India and of the Provincial Governments, whose total revenues from excise have jumped from 7½ crores of rupees in 1903–04 to nearly 21 crores in 1923–24. This Governmental "profiteering" at the expense of the vitality and morals of the people is another illustration of "unworthy trusteeship."

Before the Joint Select Committee on the Government of India Bill Sir James (now Lord) Meston said: "After the reforms the natural and inevitable course of the policy of the Ministers in dealing with excise will be to press more and more for Prohibition. They believe, rightly or wrongly, that our excise policy has encouraged intemperance among certain classes, and they are committed, deeply committed, to breaking down that policy, and to reducing the facilities for intoxicants." Lord Meston further predicted that any heroic excise policy initiated by the Ministers of Transferred Subjects would be vetoed by the Government official in control of finance, a reserved subject, and his prediction has been verified by the results. In plain parlance, British officials hold the reins, and block the path of temperance reform, as well as of sanitary and educational reform.

The solution of the drink evil, as well as of the other problems of India, therefore, depends upon self-government. As Sir Basil Blackett, the Finance Minister, and the Government of India make such a formidable weapon of the difficulty of finding alternative schemes of taxation to make good the loss of revenue which would ensue from Prohibition, surely the least they can do is to resign and allow the Swarajists and Independents—who constitute a majority in the Assembly—to form a Government and find the ways and means to finance the country under Prohibition.

"You almost persuade me to be a Swarajist," declared the Secretary of State, with the air of Pontius Pilate, "but what evidence can be adduced to back up the contention that Swaraj would inaugurate Prohibition?"

In September, 1925, after a full-dress debate in the All India Legislative Assembly, when Sir Basil Blackett, on behalf of the Government, made a very good devil's advocate of the liquor trade and the policy of the Government towards it, the following resolution was passed, sixty-nine voting for it and thirty-nine against:

"This Assembly recommends to the Governor-General in Council that he be pleased to accept as the ultimate policy of the Government the prohibition of production, manufacture, sale and import of intoxicating liquors, save for medicinal and scientific purposes. It further recommends that as the first step in carrying out this policy the Provincial Governments be directed immediately (1) to inaugurate a policy of vesting power of fixing, by a system of Local Option, the location and number of shops selling intoxicating liquors in either local self-governing bodies or licensing boards especially constituted for the purpose and elected on a popular franchise, and (2) to undertake the necessary legislation in furtherance of that policy."

The sixty-nine members consisted of the non-officials with the electors of India behind them, while twenty-five of the minority were British members of the Assembly and fourteen Indian members officially connected with the Government. Given a free hand, many of the Indian officials would probably also have voted with the majority.

The Bombay Legislative Council has approved of a policy of Prohibition to be reached in twenty years by the rationing of liquor.

The Punjab Legislative Council passed a Local Option law, which came into force in 1924, empowering municipalities and district boards to reduce the number of shops selling country liquors, but which does not apply to shops selling foreign liquors, clubs, hotels and railway refreshment rooms. The United Provinces have set up licensing boards in the large cities. In the Legislative Council of the Central Provinces a resolution in favour of Prohibition was successfully moved in 1921. In the Councils of Madras, Bombay, and Bihar and Orissa, Indian non-official members have been refused sanction by the respective Governors of these Provinces to introduce Local Option Bills, and when Colonel Wedgwood questioned the propriety of these actions in the House of Commons Earl Winterton, the Under-Secretary of State for India, declared that the Governors had acted within their statutory powers, and that there was no obligation on their part to give even reasons for their refusals.

As a stickler for constitutional practice, Lord Birkenhead rubbed his eyes and referred to section 80c of the Government of India Act, which states that a member cannot introduce any measure in any Provincial Legislative Council affecting the revenue without sanction of the Governor. "Ah," exclaimed his lordship, "I understand their reasons for refusal, for if liquor shops were shut up under Local Option by the expressed will of the people, then the revenues from drink would go down. You say the total annual revenue from drink for British India amounts to 20 to 21 crores of rupees. What are the figures for the Provinces ? "

" In 1923–24 39·9 per cent. of the total revenue of Madras was derived from drink ; 34·7 for Bihar and Orissa ; 28·7 for Bombay. including Sind ; 28·7 for Assam ; 25·3 for Central Provinces ; 20·6 for Bengal ; 13·9 for Burma ; 12·7 for United Provinces ; and 11·4 for Punjab."

" Serious percentages," mused his lordship, " but still more serious constitutional and political issues, for in the end it is Governor *versus* People. When the Governor exercises his right of veto, he robs the Legislature and the people of their rights. The whole thing is absurd as well as dangerous, for it must alienate public opinion and convince Indians that the reforms are not a step forward to responsible government, but a step backward, and consequently encourage them in their policy of Non-Co-operation. All governors have not exercised this veto ? " queried the noble lord.

" No, some do and some don't. For instance, Viscount Willingdon, when Governor of Madras, sanctioned the introduction of a Local Option Bill in 1921 in the Madras Legislative Council, and four years later Lord Goschen, the new Governor of Madras, refused the same thing."

" A Constitution which embodies such inconsistencies is crazy," cried his lordship, really exasperated, " and should be instantly revised, but how can I revise it according to my ideals, with the bureaucracy to right of me, and the Tory party to left of me, and the House of Lords behind me all the time to kick me ? "

Tout ou rien as the French say—all or nothing—should be your lordship's motto. *Toujours* courage

Always courage! A plunge into the sea of liberty will refresh and strengthen your lordship to throw off the mephitic environment in which you live. Remember Disraeli, who stole the Whigs' clothes while bathing and made the Tory party pass franchise reforms greater than his opponents. Remember Gladstone, who engendered the animosity and hatred of your party by championing Home Rule for Ireland, which your party finally participated in effecting. Remember Campbell-Bannerman's greatest feat, when he swam the ocean of imperial reaction and carried self-government safely to South Africa. On the bead-roll of fame your lordship may stand alongside these giants in the fight for freedom by revising the crazy Constitution of India on Indianised and democratic lines.

The Opium Traffic

Parliament's Condemnations

Extract from report of special House of Commons Committee, 1847, on commercial relations with China:—

"The demoralising influences of the opium trade are incontestable and inseparable from its existence."

Resolutions in the House of Commons.

April 10th, 1891. *Carried by a majority of* 30.

"That this House is of opinion that *the system by which the Indian opium revenue is raised is morally indefensible,* and would urge upon the Indian Government that it should cease to grant licences for the cultivation of the poppy and the sale of opium in British India, except to supply the legitimate demand for medicinal purposes, and that they should at the same time take measures to arrest the transit of Malwa opium through British territory."

May 30th, 1906. *Carried unanimously.*[1]

"That this House reaffirms its conviction that *the Indo-Chinese opium traffic is morally indefensible*, and requests His Majesty's Government to take such steps as may be necessary for bringing it to a speedy close."

May 6th, 1908. *Carried unanimously.*

"That this House, having regard to its resolution unanimously adopted on 30th May, 1906, that *the Indo-Chinese opium trade is morally indefensible*, welcomes the action of His Majesty's Government in their arrangement for the suppression of the consumption of the drug in that empire, and this House also urges His Majesty's Government to take steps to bring to a speedy close the system of licensing opium dens now prevailing in some of our Crown colonies, more particularly Hong Kong, the Straits Settlements and Ceylon."

In defiance of the repeated condemnation of Parliament and in defiance of Indian public opinion, the traffic in opium still flourishes in India, albeit to a somewhat slighter degree, under the auspices and approval of the Government of India.

While the Governments of America, Japan, Australia, New Zealand, Canada and South Africa, etc., have enacted prohibitive legislation of the most stringent character in order to suppress this evil, and while the League of Nations endeavours to solve this world

[1] The writer seconded the 1906 resolution.

problem, the Government of India, along with the Governments of Persia, Turkey, Russian Turkestan, Macedonia, Afghanistan and China, cultivates the poppy and manufactures the drug on a scale far beyond the medicinal requirements of the world.

How far the Government of India flouts world opinion, as well as British and Indian opinion, may be measured by the "means of demoralisation," to use Lord Palmerston's phrase, which it supplies to the world on the one hand and to the people of India on the other. The total number of chests[1] of opium exported from India in 1923 was 8,544: to Singapore, 2,100; to Hong Kong, 240; to Colombo, 30; to Batavia, 900; to Bangkok, 1,600; to Saigon, 2,975; to other places, 699; a notable decrease on 1913, when 15,760 chests were exported. In India the consumption of opium in 1923–24 was 7,406 maunds, as against 12,530 maunds in 1910–11, a decline from 27 grains per head per annum to about 18.

The net revenue to the Indian national exchequer from the sale of opium fell from an average of £4,000,000 sterling to £2,000,000 in 1919–20 and 2,24,00,00 rupees in 1925–26.

The mentality of the Government of India with regard to this traffic, which the House of Commons condemned as "morally indefensible," may be gauged by the fact that these declines in the export and internal consumption of opium seemed to it to justify its policy of "diminution" instead of "prohibition."

Speaking in the Legislative Assembly in March, 1925, the Finance Member, Sir Basil Blackett, illuminated this mentality—non-moral or immoral, let the reader judge—in the following words: "The Government do

[1] A chest contains 140 lb. of opium.

not wish to secure revenue out of the degradation of other countries, but they do not see that they are going to help forward any useful work if they themselves suddenly or even over a period of years, without co-operation from elsewhere, deprive India of her revenue and the cultivators of their employment by refusing to send exports of opium to countries whose Governments continue to license their import, in pursuance of the policy of gradual reduction, since the only result, so far as the Government of India can see, of such action on their part would be to mulct the Indian taxpayer in a considerable sum of money and have no effect whatsoever on the amount of opium imported to and consumed in these places.

" It may be said that the Government of India themselves say that opium smoking is an evil ; they ought, therefore, to prohibit the export of opium to any country where it is likely to be smoked, even though that country may get opium in equal quantities from elsewhere.

" If that is the policy which it is desired the Government of India should adopt, it is one which, I think, ought to be carefully weighed and very carefully considered by this House and by the country generally before it is adopted. It is not, as far as I can see, likely to be a useful contribution to the world problem."

On the financial point the writer had an interview with Sir E. N. Baker, the Finance Secretary of the Indian Viceregal Council, in 1907, who used the same language which he had used to the Chinese statesman Tong Shao-yi, that " the Indian Government could well dispense with the revenue they got from opium," and in speaking on the Budget he said : " When it is remembered how uncertain the opium revenue is, and how liable to violent fluctuations from causes over which we have no control, the dwindling away of its relative importance in our fiscal system must be regarded as a matter for lively satisfaction."

The cultivator will not weep when he is compelled by law to replace poppies by cereals or cotton.

On the great moral issue Archbishop Temple answers Sir Basil Blackett when he says:—

"As a Christian man I feel, and I have no doubt that a good many others feel, that we are bound to protest against the application of such principles to the national conduct, because the question has been treated very much on this footing: that, if a change in our practice cannot be proved to be certain of producing the results of diminishing the evil habit of opium smoking in China (and elsewhere), we are therefore quite at liberty to go on encouraging the evil habit, and that the moral responsibility is taken from us because, even if we discontinue what we have been doing, the result would be just the same.

"I cannot understand why any Christian man can say that he is at liberty to take any part whatever in doing a great evil on the ground that if he does not do it, it will, nevertheless, be done by other people. (Applause.) Our Lord has remarked in one place—and what He says ought certainly to be constantly present to our minds—that it is quite true that offences must come; that is, there will be temptations, and there will be stumbling blocks, and they are sure to come; but He forestalled this argument immediately by saying, 'Woe to that man by whom the offence cometh.' It will not do for you to say, 'If I do not tempt these people, the people, nevertheless, will be tempted.' If you argue in that way you are to understand, 'Woe to those who in this way bring temptation into the way of their fellow-creatures, and plead simply that they are doing what would be done by others.'"

The Times leading article of December 3rd, 1842, stated: "We think it of the highest moment that the Government of Great Britain should wash its hands once and for all, not only of all diplomatic, but of all moral and practical, responsibility for this (the opium) traffic; that we should cease to be mixed up with it, to foster it, or to make it a source of Indian revenue.

" . . . We owe some moral compensation to China for pillaging her towns and slaughtering her citizens in a quarrel which never could have arisen if we had not been guilty of *this national crime.*"

We have almost washed our hands of this *national crime* so far as China is concerned, for, with the exception of Hong Kong, we no longer export opium to China, but should we not also wash our hands of a crime against Ceylon, Singapore, Batavia, Bangkok, Saigon and India?

In India there are 17,000 licensed shops where opium can be purchased as easily as tobacco, and, unfortunately, the ravages of this powerful drug on the health and morals of its adult victims have descended upon the children through the employment of women on a larger scale in the factories. Miss Spaull, who has made careful investigations on this social evil, writes: "According to medical statistics, 98 per cent. of the mothers in the cotton factories regularly dope their babies (with opium) before going out to work."

To remove this stain on British rule in India, "we should cease to be mixed up with this traffic in opium, to foster it, or to make it a source of Indian revenue";

and, if need be, Great Britain should compensate India for the wrong done in the past by financial assistance for several years to come.

Since the above was written a Memorandum of the League of Nations, dated November 11th, 1926, indicates that a happy change has come over the policy of the Government of India, which decided on March 16th, 1926, to reduce its export of opium by 10 per cent. annually till it was extinguished, except for strictly medical purposes. The reduction begins in 1927. The sale of opium at public auction was discontinued in April, 1926. A conference of excise officers met at Simla in September, 1926, to consider ways of reducing the sale of opium in India for eating.

The Memorandum states that "this action of the Government of India has been prompted in part by League criticism, in part by the anti-opium movement among Swarajists, in part by the dubious effect of Government opium shops, whose deálers strive too hard to enlarge their *clientèle.*"

While welcoming this volteface on the part of the Government of India, the writer asks, in the words of *The Times*, Why take ten years to wash out a national crime, and why not let the Swarajists do the good work?

Betting

Betting has become so ingrained as a national vice in Great Britain that British people, even those who call themselves Christians, only smile superiorly when Indians complain that British rule is a great corrupting influence in India, fostering the evils of betting as well as of alcoholism and narcotism.

Horse-racing and betting are importations from the

West, which have grown apace in India under the patronage of Viceroys, Governors, Prelates and Indian Princes. "The betting evil has spread from the idle rich to the commercial communities, the middle classes, the labourers working in factories and the schoolboys. Over and above thousands of people regularly going to the races week after week, there are thousands more to whom temptation to gamble comes in the shape of bucket-shops, openly plying their trade in the heart of the city."

How many thousands a year are ruined by this fashionable vice, at which the British governors connive, God only knows! Under British rule there is little or no hope for the moral and material progress of India, while under Indian rule these pests of betting, alcoholism and opium-eating and opium-smoking would be destroyed.

If Gandhi were Viceroy, India would give England lessons in moral and material progress, and in nation-building.

CHAPTER XII

EDUCATION

AFTER almost a century and a half of British rule India is still without a national system of education, is still without a national system of training colleges for teachers, is still without a national system of schools for children, is still without free and compulsory education. In 1870 England by Act of Parliament recognised that education formed the foundation stone of national life and national greatness, that education was the birthright of every child, poor or rich, and that the first duty of the State was to provide a school place for every child, male or female. Scotland, of course, with its higher ideals and greater appreciation of knowledge, had a national system of education long before England, and yet England and Scotland in their governance of India have failed all these precious years to provide the facilities for the most elementary knowledge, for lack of which the silent masses of India perish.

How great has been the failure may be measured in the amount of illiteracy amongst the people—91·8 per cent. were illiterate in 1921, comprising 86·1 per cent. of the male population and 97·9 per cent. of the female—and in the fact that education is the first need of agricultural and industrial development, of economic and political emancipation, and of the drawing out of the noblest and the best in the life of the individual and the nation. How egregiously we have failed may be gathered from the conclusion of Sir Michael Sadler's Commission in 1919, which Sir Valentine Chirol sums up as follows: "Efficiency was the watchword of the administrative era ushered in by the transfer of India to the Crown after the Mutiny. . . . But the one thing that era utterly failed to produce was any coherent educational system, even in respect of higher education, on which the energies of Government were almost wholly concentrated."

In spite of Sir Charles Wood's famous despatch of 1854, in which he urged the Government to create a system of education leading up from the elementary schools to the Indian universities, "the Sadler Commission still looked in vain three-quarters of a century later" for any system; and in spite of the recommendations of Lord Ripon's Commission in 1882 to establish primary education, the Government of India continued to neglect the foundation of education—the primary school—and to concentrate on the secondary schools and the universities. It looks as if fear to educate the masses, its future masters, dictated this policy of the Government of India, as it dictated the same policy of the Tory party towards education of the masses in England prior to 1870.

From neglect of popular education the Government descended to opposition to Indian private efforts to establish Indian schools and colleges. Lord Curzon, the most reactionary Governor-General of India of modern times and "a great autocrat with an overwhelming faith in the efficiency of Government machinery," in the words of Sir Valentine Chirol, became alarmed at this sign of independence on the part of Indians in providing their own educational facilities free from Government control, and he passed the Indian Universities Act of 1904, by which (1) 80 per cent. of the members of the Senate were to be Government nominees, and the Governor of the Province in which the University was situated was to be the *ex-officio* Chancellor of the University; (2) the regulations regarding public schools were tightened up, minimum fees insisted upon, and free studentships reduced.

"Indian opinion, which Lord Curzon made no serious attempt to consult, protested against such a comprehensive scheme of officialisation, and in Calcutta especially, where the large majority of the Senate consisted of Indians, the Act was attacked as a political blow deliberately aimed at its independence. The Viceroy was accused of wishing to strangle Western education, because the new generation of Indians it had produced possessed the courage and ability to criticise and oppose him. The heated controversy over the Act was the forerunner of the fierce outburst which the partition of Bengal was about to provoke, and Lord Curzon left India before there was time to carry out the more beneficial features of a reforms scheme which in any case failed to strike at the roots of the evil," are the observations of Sir Valentine Chirol upon this Act.

The Indian National Congress at its annual meetings passed resolutions demanding the introduction of free and compulsory education, and in 1911 Mr. Gokhale, the able leader of the Moderate party, failed to carry a Bill for free and compulsory primary education through the Imperial Legislative Council, the Government rejecting it on the grounds that "the time has not yet come for such a measure," "funds are not available to meet the necessary expenses," and "the masses are opposed to compulsion," lame excuses which only exposed the Government to the charge that they were "fraudulent trustees" of the children, for the Indian State of Baroda had given its boys and girls free and compulsory education for nearly twenty years, and likewise the Indian States of Mysore and Travancore.

In 1916 Mr. V. J. Patel, the present President of the Legislative Assembly, endeavoured to give power to the local authorities to introduce free and compulsory education, but the official majority in the Bombay Provincial Council voted out his Bill, because it would be in violation of the policy of the Government of India.

Since 1921 education has been a "transferred" subject in the hands of Ministers responsible to the Provincial Legislatures, but the efforts towards free and compulsory elementary education have been damped down by the paralysing parsimony of British Ministers of "Finance"—a "reserved" subject—over whom the Legislatures have no control.

Regarding higher education, the report of the Sadler Commission points out the mistakes made by British rulers, and Sir Valentine Chirol, who has written a book on India which is largely an apology for British rule, cannot refrain from making the following criticisms :—

"Education was conceived almost exclusively in terms of a literary education. . . . Young Indians needed even more than British youths the wholesome intellectual discipline of a science course. . . . Instruction assumed a more and more mechanical character. . . . The teachers were discouraged and the students led astray by a system which tended to make examinations the be-all and the end-all of education. . . . The heart was taken out of the Indian members of the

Educational Service by its reorganisation on a basis of almost flagrant *racial discrimination*[1] to their detriment. . . . Indians found themselves relegated to an inferior pen. . . . A bureaucratic atmosphere is generally deadening, and never more than where education is concerned. . . . The university standards of instruction had to be gradually lowered. . . . Though Indian boys were pushed, often at too early a stage, to acquire some knowledge of English, as the university courses were in English, they seldom learnt enough to be able to follow them with any understanding ; and as they had not been taught their own vernacular, they were left without any language in which they could learn to think. They were thrown back on learning by heart. . . . They were expected to assimilate through the medium of a foreign language a whole order of new ideas equally foreign to that in which they had been brought up in their own homes. This is one of the inherent difficulties of Western education in India, even when conducted on the most approved lines. . . . For occupations involving manual labour their education had rarely done anything to train them. . . . They could not bear the prospect of returning to the drudgery of their humble homes. . . . They formed an intellectual proletariat ripe for any mischief, and the crashing of their hopes embittered them towards an alien system that had caught them in its toils and then cast them out on to the streets, and towards the alien *raj* which they held responsible for it. . . . It was also inevitable that when the best young Indian minds were fed upon the masterpieces of English literature, and when the history of English social and political evolution taught

[1] The italics are mine.

them to seek the secret of England's greatness in her ancient love and achievement of freedom, they should have begun to apply all these lessons to the condition of their own country, . . . to apply them to criticism of an alien system of government and to gratify the aspirations to freedom which their receptive minds have absorbed from Burke and Shelley and Byron and Mill, and all the Western apostles of democracy, by preaching the liberation of the Indian nation, as their vivid imagination conceives it, from an alien and therefore oppressive yoke. . . . Can a new type be born of men alone without the co-operation of women? That co-operation Western education has barely ever enlisted. . . . Even in Western countries the State has been slow to recognise the importance of including girls as well as boys in any educational system that is to build up a nation. It was still more tardily recognised in India. . . . The provision of adequate training colleges for an Indian teaching staff had been gravely neglected. . . . A very serious impediment to the teaching of girls is the dearth of women teachers. . . . The greatest source of weakness was the lack of any solid substance of elementary education."

In view of the above catalogue of criticisms, the reader may reasonably ask whether the introduction of English as the medium of learning and of Western education into the colleges and universities of India was not the worst blunder ever committed under British rule. British Imperialists, who are unfaithful to British ideals of freedom, and who want to keep India in bondage, will unhesitatingly answer "Yes," because in their opinion English and English ideals have been a unifying influence in India, helping to make India a united nation.

Sir Valentine Chirol, who is more faithful to British ideas of freedom and justice, and who recognises India's title to self-determination, answers: "Western education cannot be called a failure when it has produced an intellectual *élite* capable of playing such a part as it does to-day in modern India. It has shown that Indian brains, when given a fair chance, are no whit inferior to European brains. Indians have succeeded in wrestling with and overcoming the tremendous initial difficulty of learning everything through a foreign tongue."

But important as these points of view may be, they sink into comparative insignificance beside those of Mahatma Gandhi, who speaks for India and her silent masses. "In my opinion," Gandhi writes, "the existing system of education is defective, apart from its association with an utterly unjust Government, in three most important matters: (1) It is based upon foreign culture to the almost entire exclusion of indigenous culture. (2) It ignores the culture of the heart and the hand, and confines itself simply to the head. (3) Real education is impossible through a foreign medium. . . . A boy is never taught to have any pride in his surroundings. The higher he goes the farther he is removed from his home, so that at the end of his education he becomes estranged from his surroundings. . . . His own civilisation is presented to him as imbecile, barbarous, superstitious and useless for all practical purposes. . . . If the mass of educated youths are not entirely denationalised, it is because the ancient culture is too deeply embedded in them. . . . If I had my way I would certainly destroy the majority of the present text-books, and cause to be written text-books which have a bearing on and correspondence with the home life, so that a boy as he learns may react upon his immediate surroundings. . . . In India, where more than 80 per cent. of the population is agricultural and 10 per cent. industrial, it is a crime to make education merely literary, and to unfit boys and girls for manual work. . . . Our children must be taught the dignity of labour. . . . Manual training will serve a double purpose in a poor country like ours; it will pay for the education of our children and teach them an occupation. . . . The foreign medium has caused brain fag, put an undue strain on the nerves of our children, made them crammers and imitators, unfitted them for original work and thought, and disabled them for filtrating their learning to the family or the masses. The foreign medium has made our children practically foreigners in their own land. It is the greatest tragedy of the existing system. It has prevented the growth of our vernaculars. If I had the powers of a despot, I would to-day stop the tuition of our boys and girls through a foreign medium. . . . I regard English as the language of international commerce and diplomacy, and therefore consider its knowledge on the part of some of us as essential. As it contains some of the richest treasures of thought and literature, I would encourage its careful study among those who have linguistic talents, and expect them to translate these treasures for the nation in its vernaculars. Nothing can be further from my thought than that we should become exclusive or erect barriers, but I contend that an appreciation of other cultures can fitly follow, never precede, an appreciation and assimilation of our own. It is my firm opinion that no culture has treasures so rich as ours has."

Suiting the action to the word, Gandhi established

a university and college at Ahmedabad to carry out his ideals, as we related in another chapter.

There are fifteen universities in India, namely, Calcutta, Madras, Bombay, Punjab, Allahabad, Benares (Hindu); Mysore, Patna, Osmania (Hyderabad), Dacca, Aligarh (Muslim); Lucknow, Delhi, Nagpur and Rangoon (Burma).

The Shreemati Thackeray Indian Women's University was started in 1915 under private auspices, and the Lady Hardinge Medical College for Women at Delhi is training many Indian women for medical service.

The popular cry in India to-day is for elementary education, and, so far as the Government of India is concerned, it is like one crying in the wilderness.

CHAPTER XIII

INDIAN STATES

India may be divided into two parts: British India, for which we are entirely responsible, and Indian States, for which we are indirectly responsible. Numbering nearly 700, Indian States cover more than one-third of the whole area of India and nearly a quarter of the total population.

They present three different types:—

1. Fully powered States, with complete rights of making laws and of civil and criminal jurisdiction.
2. States whose civil and criminal jurisdiction and power of making laws are under the control of the Government of India through its agent.
3. Congeries of States like Kathiawar (which comprises 143 States), Bundelkund and Simla Hills, which have only inferior jurisdiction, and are without treaty rights enjoyed by the two previous classes.

About 100 States fall under the first two categories, their princes being entitled to "Their Highness" and a salute of at least eleven guns, whilst the princes of the rest of the States are without these privileges.

In external matters Indian States have no standing, India forming from an international point of view a complete unity, although they had representatives on the war councils during the war and at the Peace Conference at Paris, and also on the League of Nations, but the Government of India has consistently declared that the prince whom they select represents the Government of India and not the princes. British India is also represented on the League, but the representative is a Government nominee, and not elected, as he ought to be, by the Legislative Assembly.

In regard to internal affairs, the major States, like Hyderabad, Gwalior, Mysore, Travancore, Baroda, etc., govern themselves, whilst the minor States are practically governed by the agents of the Government of India. When questions like railways, customs, posts and telegraphs, which affect all India, arise, the interests of India naturally take precedence.

The policy of the Government of India in regard to the minor Indian States is more often inexplicable than not. In some cases it interferes too much and in others too little. There are examples of ruling chiefs being honoured by Government who have a bad record morally and administratively, and who have put heavy burdens on their people by contracting debts for the gratification of their personal caprices. It looks as if the loyalty of individual rulers to the Government of India, and not the people's welfare and the public good, determined the attitude of the paramount power to the Indian States.

Politically the Indian States exhibit various stages of evolution, the vast majority being old Oriental autocracies, in which the rulers treat the State revenue as their private purse, while a few, such as Mysore, Travancore, Baroda, etc., have followed in the wake of British India and created Legislative Councils, which are more or less of the same character as those conferred on British India by the British Parliament; that is to say that their powers are mainly consultative. Eventually the final decision lies with the princes or ruling chiefs, as in the case of British governors in British India. In a few advanced States a civil list has been established.

In the education of the masses the rulers of the Indian States of Travancore, Baroda and Mysore have beaten the rulers of British India. Some other States recently have provided free and compulsory education.

Among the Indian States which the writer visited Mysore may be taken as one of the best governed and most progressive in the whole of India. The head of the State is the Maharajah, in whom all power is ultimately concentrated. His Highness appoints his own Prime Minister, the Dewan, and the members of his own Executive Council, three or four in number. As in British India, the Constitution is bicameral, consisting of the Legislative Council, with fifty members, twenty of whom are officials, and the Representative Assembly, with 250 members, elected on what in England would be considered a narrow franchise. Women have recently been admitted as voters. The powers of these councils are chiefly consultative, and there is a strong agitation in the State to convert them into real parliamentary institutions based on the will of the people, as expressed by a popular franchise. The Dewan is *ex-officio* President of both the Representative Assembly and the Legislative Council. There is a civil list. The position and powers of the British Resident, who represents the Government of India, are difficult to define. By some he would be regarded as an ambassador, and by others as the *deus ex machinâ*.

Educationally Mysore is far ahead of British India. Its university combines both teaching and residential departments, with well-equipped and well-staffed engineering and medical colleges, a training college for teachers, and the Maharani's college for women. The wonderful Indian Institute of Science for research work at Bangalore, founded by the munificence of the Tata family, deserves special mention. The main feature, however, is that primary education is compulsory and free, and the children are provided with schools and instruction, including agricultural, commercial, engineering and other technical subjects.

State Socialism in Mysore has advanced beyond the pioneer stage in the successful manufacture of sandalwood oil, charcoal, pig-iron, and in the development of electric energy from waterfalls.

A great grievance of the Mysore State against the Government of India is the compulsory contribution of 35 lakhs a year towards the upkeep of the British Army in India, in addition to the annual cost of the Mysore Army, amounting to 21 lakhs. Both British India and the Indian States groan under the financial burden of British militarism.

The political ferment produced by the Great War "to make the world safe for democracy" has not only pervaded British India, but also the Indian (native) States. Theoretically the day of the Divine right of princes and of conquerors to treat their subjects as chattels and slaves is gone, even in the most backward parts of India, hitherto accustomed to paternal and tyrannical government.

The people in the Indian States as well as in British India have awakened to the rights of men to rule themselves, and the Die-hards of autocracy and bureaucracy who oppose democratic institutions and the will of the people are only inviting trouble for themselves and India.

With regard to this rapidly growing demand for self-government in the major States, the Government of India is between the devil and the deep sea, for parliamentary government in Indian States would be a sharp reflection upon unparliamentary government in British India, and would restrict and abolish British authority in Indian States.

The Chamber of Princes, over which the Viceroy presides, holds its sessions with closed doors, and its proceedings are not published, so that the natural inference is that it serves no useful purpose beyond being a sort of glorified trade union for the protection of princes. Indian opinion regards this Chamber as a counterpoise to the reformed councils, as a sop to Indian princes on the doctrine of "Divide and rule."

When the British Government was busy Constitution-mongering, one wonders why it forgot to create at the same time a Chamber of Deputies for the Indian States as a set-off to the Chamber of Princes. Of course such action might have been interpreted in high quarters as gross interference with the sacred principles of self-government so far as princes are concerned, but what about the sacred principles of self-government applied to the people in the Indian States? Are they not entitled to consideration? A *plebiscite* would reveal their wishes, whether they desire to continue to crawl under and sometimes to be crushed under autocratic government or to walk erect under parliamentary government. At the same time a *plebiscite* might be taken in British India as to whether the people are satisfied with the 1919 Constitution or whether they want complete parliamentary government.

Not only were the Indian States entirely neglected by Parliament when it drew up the ramshackle Constitution of 1919, but the All India Legislative Assembly was precluded, and has been precluded under the rules of debate, from discussing vital questions affecting the common interests of Indian States and British India, even the States that are managed by British administrators appointed by the British Government on behalf of the minor chiefs. The Montford Report recognised the need of instituting an organisation wherein the representatives of British Indiá and those of the Indian States would sit together and deliberate, but the Coalition Government was too cowardly to contemplate a Federated India.

The failure of British statesmanship in 1919 has done incalculable harm to India, and seriously impeded her evolution towards federation. To keep up the division of India into two parts is inimical to every interest of India and to world progress. Federation must come and will come, despite the selfish barrage of Indian princes and British bureaucrats; federation, in fact, already exists in an inchoate form in matters of defence, foreign policy, etc.

A Federated India demands immediate revision of the Constitution on a democratic basis. Meanwhile the Government of India might prepare the ground by inaugurating a consistent policy regarding the Indian States in the directions (1) of insisting upon a minimum of constitutional government, (2) of limiting the civil list, and (3) of establishing certain fundamental popular rights, such as freedom from arbitrary arrest, non-interference with judicial proceedings, and freedom from confiscation of property, etc.

In the interests of princes, it ought to be made clear that their future would be more assured if they were in the position of "constitutional monarchs," carrying out the will of the people through parliamentary government, instead of being autocrats.

The Right Hon. Srinivasa Sastri answers the question, What about the treaties between the British and the princes? "The Indian States had better be warned in time: our rajahs and maharajahs will find that the British crown, having done full justice to its own Indian subjects (when responsible government is granted), will rather sympathise with the struggling subjects of the States than feel compelled by the terms of out-of-date treaties to raise their strong arms in support of mediæval despotisms."

CHAPTER XIV

BRITISH IMPERIAL EXCUSES FOR DELAYING SELF-GOVERNMENT FOR INDIA ; LORD BIRKENHEAD ANSWERED

THE two main excuses of British Imperialists for refusing Indians the inalienable right to rule themselves and for Great Britain to continue politically to strangle India are, that under the benign and beneficent influence of Home Rule India would be torn to pieces by internal or external strife or both.

The real reason for refusing Swaraj is never mentioned now in public places like the Houses of Parliament, although the writer well remembers the truth being blurted out in the House of Commons several years ago that " we hold India for Lancashire."

Lord Birkenhead repudiated in part that honest confession when he said in the House of Lords in July, 1925 : " We no longer talk of holding *the gorgeous East in fee.*" But his illustrious predecessor, the late Lord Salisbury, did not mince matters when he used the words " India must be bled."

The Marquis of Salisbury contradicts Lord Birkenhead, who tries to make the world believe that finance does not rule the world, that finance does not rule England, that finance does not rule India.

In India this reason is recognised, and when Lord Birkenhead claims trusteeship Indians reply, " Yes, England is the trustee for British capitalism." This vital truth settled, we may now consider the imperial excuses.

Lord Birkenhead, equipped with the latest bombs made in the India Office, excelled himself when he told the assembled lords that " if we withdrew from India to-morrow the immediate consequences would be a struggle *à outrance* between the Moslems and the Hindu population." So panic-stricken were their lordships by this *brutum fulmen* that one can readily conceive them holding a private conclave afterwards without reporters, when the following *imaginary debate* took place :—

" You don't really mean it ? " queried their lordships of the Chief Secretary. " You were just roaring like a lion or an *ignis fatuus* to frighten the British people, in order to prevent them keeping the solemn oath of Parliament that Indians shall govern India, but please don't frighten us too, for our nerves are none too strong, since we fought in the Great War and made the world safe for democracy."

" Be careful," stammered a noble lord. " You, and Montagu, and Chelmsford, and Lloyd George, and our dear departed Bonar Law should have thought of that before you promised Indians responsible government."

" It would scarcely be playing the game to make a molehill into a mountain," whispered another earl, with bated breath. He had served his country as Governor of the Punjab, and knew a thing or two more than the Secretary of State, whom he warned in the following language : " Beware ! You are treading on dangerous ground, for Indians will remind us that Hindus and Moslems don't half knock each other about like Dyer and O'Dwyer knocked Hindus and Moslems about. One Jallianwalla Bagh will wipe out all the casualties of fifty years' riots between Moslems and Hindus."

" For God's sake, Birkenhead," cried an irate Irish nobleman, " put a bridle on your tongue, and remember that Catholics and Protestants in Ireland used to cudgel and fire each other under British rule, and, now that British rule has gone, live and work together in peace, thinking only of their country's good. You cannot honestly use this argument of Hindu-Moslem fracas against Home Rule for India any more than the Catholic-Protestant antagonism against Home Rule for Ireland."

A pious pillar of the Church then prayed silence for a moment while he drew his lordship's attention to the facts that Christians of different denominations used to burn each other at the stake, hypocritically giving God the glory, and that in the recent war Christians not only killed each other in what is called legitimate warfare, but killed each other's women and children in illegitimate and still more devilish warfare. In these circumstances were Christians justified in criticising Hindus and Moslems, who occasionally hit each other with sticks and stones, and had we any right to withhold self-government from them ? Let him that is without sin cast the first stone.

" As for the assertion," added another lord, " that ' in these dissensions we have kept our hands unsullied by partnership,' my noble friend seems to have forgotten the speech of Sir Bampfylde Fuller, when Governor of Bengal, that he had two wives, Hindu and Moslem, and that the Moslem was his favourite. Did not Lord Curzon, as Viceroy, flout Hindu opinion by the Partition of Bengal in the hope of winning favour with Moslems ? And, worst of all, did not the introduction of ' communal electorates ' by the Government of England aggravate and intensify Hindu-Moslem rivalry ? Indians have no doubt in their minds that British policy has always been 'Divide and rule,' the historic policy of conquerors throughout the ages."

. . . . .

When the writer drew Mahatma Gandhi's attention to Lord Birkenhead's outburst, and its effect on British public opinion, he asked me to assure my countrymen that when Britain withdraws from India Hindus and Moslems will not kill each other to the same extent that Englishmen have killed Hindus and Moslems, that Indians will not indulge in civil war, that India will not have a War of the Roses, and that Hindus and Moslems will compose their differences amicably.

Mr. Jinnah, the distinguished leader of the Mohammedans in the Legislative Assembly, informed the writer that the historical answer to Lord Birkenhead's contention was Canada, where the differences between English and French were on a much bigger and more serious scale than those between Hindus and Moslems in India. Whereas the differences between Hindus and Moslems were chiefly confined to religion, which many of them had changed and interchanged, those between English and French extended to religion, race and language.

Hindus object to "cow-killing," and Moslems to "music in the vicinity of mosques," especially during religious service, and he would be a bold bad man who would compare these apples of discord with the bitter racial rivalry and hatred between English and French, which had been intensified on a hundred fields of battle, and in a long-drawn-out "struggle *à outrance*" for empire. To appreciate these antagonisms and rivalries, their scope and permeation, in the private and public life of Canada, their dividing, disintegrating and disastrous influence on the peace, progress and prosperity of Canada, one should re-read Lord Durham's vivid and enlightening report.

Canada's ills were cured by the granting of full representative and responsible government, when all the icy differences of race, religion and language melted away before the sun of a common freedom and a common patriotism.

Are the religious differences of Hindus and Moslems comparable to the rivalry and hatred between Boers and Britons, which led to a two and a half years' "struggle *à outrance*"?

When a greater man than Lord Birkenhead, when another Durham, or Campbell-Bannerman, or Keir Hardie, confers self-government on India, Hindus and Moslems will unite in a common patriotism to work out the salvation of their motherland.

Whilst recognising the gravity of the quarrels which arise occasionally and spasmodically between Hindus and Moslems, we must avoid the mistake of magnifying them onto a national scale, provocative of civil war; and, above all, we must rule them out as illegitimate excuses for postponing Swaraj on the precedent of Lord Durham, who urged self-government as the remedy for the quarrels between British and French Canadians.

Let there be no mistake or misunderstanding with regard to the hearty and unanimous agreement between Hindus and Moslems in their love for India and India's freedom from British rule under a purely Indian Government. Time and tide have brought them together: for centuries they have worked together in uninterrupted harmony in Indian States, and in harmony interrupted by a few "makes" and "breaks" in British India. Education, which the British have neglected, and responsibility in government, which the British have denied, will weld them into a perfect family, as those cementing factors did in Ireland, and Canada, and South Africa. The cobwebs of religious fanaticism are always blown away by the healthy and purifying winds of freedom, and enlightenment, and patriotism.

The second excuse of British Imperialism for treating British pledges to India as "scraps of paper" is that, if the British lion walked out of India to-day some other imperial monster would walk in to-morrow. The Caliban that would do this dirty work is not specified. It is left to the imagination to guess, whether he might come from Afghanistan, or China, or Japan, or Russia, or Italy.

Signor Mussolini is credited with vaster designs than Cæsar or Cecil Rhodes, or the deposed Kaiser, but before he got to India he would want to take Abyssinia, and Egypt, and the Suez Canal, and Aden, so that he may be dismissed with a Portia's smile.

The Indian casket is neither open to Mussolini nor to any other imperial competitor, for Indian Nationalists have not asked for Independence. They only ask for self-government "within the Empire," or, more correctly speaking, "within the British Commonwealth," with the same status as Australia and Canada. So that the imperial monster who dared to contemplate an invasion of India would have to reckon with the might of the British Commonwealth, which means that no sane Power would entertain the idea for two minutes. But, for the sake of argument, suppose the British Commonwealth of nations separated into its constituent parts, or the people of Great

Britain became so wise as to discard militarism and declined to defend India, long before that time arrived India would have organised her own defence forces, and would be capable of preserving her own freedom.

Lord Sinha, whom John Morley appointed to be the first Indian member of the Governor-General's Executive Council in 1908, and whom Lord Birkenhead has recently appointed a member of the Judicial Committee of the Privy Council, in his address as President of the Indian National Congress in 1915 said :—

"There should be a frank and full statement of the policy of the Government as regards the future of India, so that hope might come where despair holds sway, and faith where doubt spreads its darkening shadow, and that steps should be taken towards self-government by the gradual development of popular control over all departments of government, and by removal of disabilities and restrictions under which we labour, both in our own country and in other parts of the British Empire. . . . We ask for the right to enlist in the regular Army. . . . We ask that the commissioned ranks of the Indian Army should be thrown open to all classes . . . and that a military college or colleges should be established in India. . . . We ask that all classes should be allowed to join as volunteers ; . . . that the invidious distinctions under the Arms Act should be removed. . . . It is not correct to assert of any section of the Indian people that it is wanting in such physical courage and manly virtues as to render it incapable of bearing arms. But even if it were so, is it not the obvious duty of England so to train Indians as to remove this incapacity, especially if it be the case *that it is English rule that has brought them to such a pass?* England has ruled this country for over a hundred and fifty years now, and surely it cannot be a matter of pride to her at the end of this period that the withdrawal of her rule would mean chaos and anarchy, and would leave the country an easy prey to any foreign adventurers. There are some of our critics who never fail to remind us that if the English were to leave the country to-day, we would have to wire to them to come back before they got to Aden. Some even enjoy the grim joke that were the English to withdraw now, there would be neither a rupee nor a virgin left in some parts of the country. I can think of no more scathing indictment of the results of British rule. A superman might gloat over the spectacle of the conquest of might over justice and righteousness, but I am much mistaken if the British nation would consider it as other than discreditable to itself that after nearly two centuries of British rule India had been brought to-day to the same emasculated condition as that of the Britons in the beginning of the fifth century, when the Roman legions left the English shores in order to defend their own country against the Huns, Goths, and other barbarian hordes."

Indian Nationalists have never proposed that the British Army in India should march out of India the day after she enjoys Home Rule. Rightly they have demanded Indianisation of the Army they pay, which is quite a different proposition. But surely one good turn deserves another. As the Indian Army saved Great Britain in the Great War, it is up to us to leave the British section of that army in India until the All India Legislative Assembly gives the command to go, which will be within a reasonable time. Our failure to Indianise the Army forms another and a powerful reason for our guaranteeing the security of India from foreign invasion in the early days of Home Rule.

In discussing the question of guarantees for India against invasion and the hand of war, why do Imperialists systematically snub or prostitute the League of Nations? What nobler service could the League render than the protection of India from imperial "bounders"? A caveat must be entered here. There must be no question of "mandate" to Great Britain, Japan, or any other Power, for the last thing that Indians desire is to be condemned by the League of Nations under the camouflage of "mandate" to an interminable number of years of subjection to any imperial vampire. Mandated Imperialism would be more intolerable than naked Imperialism, unblushing and unabashed.

The writer has no doubt whatever that when India is allowed to raise her own army, officered by her own sons, she will be capable of defending her frontiers, and that to talk about Pathans and Afghans rushing down to overwhelm and subdue her is wild and discreditable nonsense.

As devil's advocate, Lord Birkenhead trumped up the further Tory and imperial excuses for keeping India down—namely, the number of religions and languages in India, excuses which he should have left safely buried in the vaults of the India Office, especially after committing himself and his country in 1919 to Indian self-government. In palming "nine great religions" and "130 different speeches" on the concentrated intelligence of the House of Lords, his object was evidently to prove to his peers that people indulging in so many religions and speaking so many tongues were unfit to rule themselves. When his lordship ceases to be coached by sun-dried bureaucrats and consults Mr. Gandhi, he will learn from him that "out of a population of 315 millions only 38 millions living in the Madras Presidency cannot follow a Hindustani speaker, . . . that the majority of Mohammedans of the Madras Presidency understand Hindustani, . . . that audiences outside Madras can more or less understand Hindustani without difficulty, . . . that Hindustani is a resultant of Hindu and Urdu," and that Hindustani is rapidly becoming the *lingua franca* of India.

When Lord Birkenhead acquires Hindustani and visits India he will be able to communicate his great thoughts on liberty, equality and fraternity—it would be wiser to omit those on rebellion—to the vast majority of her citizens; and if his lordship added Tamil to his repertoire, the great majority of the people of the Madras Presidency would understand him too.

His lordship should revisit the United States and tell Americans that they are unfit to govern themselves because they practise all the religions under the sun and speak numberless tongues.

While in India his lordship would learn from Indian authorities on languages that his statement of "130 different speeches" was most misleading, and should have been "different dialects," for the languages of India only number twelve: Bengali, Hindustani (Hindi), Urdu, Gujerati, Mahratti, Tamil, Telugu, Canarese, Malayalam, Cashmiri, Sindhi and Punjabi, of which the last three are dying out.

His lordship's contention that "to talk of India as an entity is as absurd as to talk of Europe as an entity" has already been answered by the Government of India erecting a new city outside Delhi, with new Houses of Parliament, and Chamber of Princes, and Administrative Buildings, at a gigantic cost to represent New India as a new entity or federation of entities. The latest answer, however, comes from Lord Reading, the ex-Viceroy, who said at the dinner given by the Federation of Chambers of Commerce of the British Empire to the members of the Imperial Conference in November, 1926 : " If it had not been for Great Britain, India would not now be a nation, but would be divided up into a series of nations according to race, creed and caste." Why does Lord Birkenhead lag behind Lord Reading in claiming that British rule has made India a nation ?

On the subject of religion and the morals and ethics of Imperialism Lord Birkenhead might sit at the feet of Mahatma Gandhi with advantage, and realise the immorality and the evil of British domination over India. It is within the region of possibility that the Mahatma might convert his lordship as he converted General Smuts. His lordship missed a great opportunity of healing the breach between England and India in 1925, when the Viceroy, Lord Reading, came over to London to confer with him. Shall it be recorded in history that, like the Bourbons, he learnt nothing and forgot nothing ?

CHAPTER XV

THE POLITICAL SITUATION

The Attitude of British Political Parties to India

India and World Progress

THE political situation in India is full of danger, for India is united, as she never was before, in her hostility to British rule, in her contempt for many aspects of British civilisation, which appear to her to be largely an alloy of gross materialism and brutal militarism, and in her determination to win self-government.

Hindus, Muslims, Sikhs, Brahmins and non-Brahmins, all sorts and conditions of men, and all the political parties are animated by one patriotic aim, the attainment of Home Rule.

The base ingratitude of England for India's services in the Great War, as revealed in the reign of repression and terror inaugurated immediately after the Armistice, and in the great swindle of the Constitution of 1919, shattered India's faith in British honesty and in Britain's intentions to fulfil the promises of "responsible government" given during the war, when England was in need of India's help.

Thanks to Mahatma Gandhi and the religious concepts of the people, this spirit of discontent and revolt has been largely kept in check, and murder or attempts at murder of British officials have been few and far between.

Paradoxical though it may appear, Gandhi is the greatest bulwark of British rule in India to-day and the best guarantee against a campaign of assassination and violence. If he ceased preaching the gospel of loving your enemies and of praying for them which despitefully use you, and withdrew his veto on violence, political crime in India would probably exceed political crime in Ireland and Italy under foreign rule, and the lot of English officials would become intolerable.

India demands a Round Table Conference to revise the Constitution in accordance with the principles embodied in the resolution passed by the All India Legislative Assembly in September, 1925. The modesty of this demand and the moderation of the principles enumerated in the resolution betoken a sweet reasonableness on the part of the elected representatives of India, which is rarely found in political life, especially under alien domination, and which stands out in vivid contrast to the stone wall attitude of the Baldwin-Birkenhead Government, a slave to dates and to tradition. Lord Birkenhead will not entertain revision of the Constitution until 1929, as specified in the Act of 1919.

When Mr. Baldwin and Lord Birkenhead talk about "goodwill and co-operation," Indian patriots are no more deceived than British miners and British workmen, for they know by experience that these beautiful words in the mouths of Tories mean "keeping things as they are," keeping the ring while British capitalism exploits them and their country.

His lordship made this perfectly clear when he said on July 7th, 1925, "I am not able in any foreseeable future to discover a moment when we may safely, either to ourselves or India, abandon our trust."

"Abandon our trust" on Tory lips is equivalent to "abandon our privileges and powers." Indians interpret this declaration as a definite betrayal of India, and as a definite abandonment of the policy of "goodwill and co-operation" decided upon by the House of Commons in 1917.

Actions speak louder than words. During two years the Baldwin-Birkenhead Government has been in power with a magnificent majority in the House of Commons and a docile House of Lords, and yet it has done nothing for India except (1) to compel her to pay her alien rulers more; (2) to insult her with a Royal Commission on Agriculture without power to inquire into the system of land tenure and land taxation, which lie at the root of agricultural depression; (3) to reject the request for a Round Table Conference; and (4) to feed "the demon of suspicion," "to expel and exorcise" which Lord Birkenhead postulated as essential to good relations and progress.

The Liberal party may or may not be as dead as the dodo, but Indians feel that since the departure of Sir Henry Campbell-Bannerman the policy of that party on imperial questions has been difficult to differentiate from that of the Tory party. Some portion of Campbell-Bannerman's mantle seemed to have fallen on Montagu, but his association with Liberal Imperialists of the calibre of Asquith, Grey and Lloyd George tore his mantle to pieces, and his coalition with Tories, the undisguised champions of Imperialism, gave the *coup de grâce* to his fine intentions of "responsible government" for India, and ended in the Montagu-Chelmsford abortion. Imperialism destroyed Liberalism in England and in Europe.

The Labour party alone is left to honour British

pledges and to bear the torch of liberty to India. Sad to relate, the Labour Government of 1924, absorbed in the problem of a European settlement, missed the opportunity of an Indian settlement. What it might have done by recalling the Viceroy and replacing him by a strong man, strong in his faith in Labour ideals for the settlement of the world, a man with the wisdom and the courage of a Durham, a man who would have opened the prison doors to all political prisoners, who would have established the courts of justice above the executive and the police, who would have laid down plans for the Indianisation of the Army and Civil Service, and who would have held a Round Table Conference for the revision of the Constitution according to Indian ideals, belongs, unfortunately, to the realm of conjecture.

No future Labour Government should enter upon the great adventure of government with the highest authorities—Viceroys and Governors—tainted with Imperialism. Labour must employ its own clean and healthy instruments for carrying out its own clean and healthy policy.

If the Labour Government had gone down with colours flying in a great effort of justice to India instead of on the Campbell case, it would have earned the respect of the people of India as well as of the people of England.

What the Labour Government did do in a moment of forgetfulness was to bend the knee to Baal, to accept the policy of Imperialism of Lord Reading, whom no member of the Labour party would follow in home affairs, and to dash the hopes and expectations, not only of Indian patriots, but of Internationalists throughout the world, who are striving for the overthrow of Imperialism and for the creation of the commonwealth of nations.

The Independent Labour party dissociated itself from the policy of the Labour Government towards India, opposed the Bengal Ordinance, and urged a Round Table Conference in the following resolution, which was passed unanimously at the annual meeting in 1924: "This conference is of opinion that the time has arrived to seek a settlement of the problem of the government of India by calling a conference of representatives of the various parties in India and inviting them to prepare a scheme of self-government for discussion with the British Government with a view to immediate application."

When Lord Olivier outraged Indian opinion and British Labour by sanctioning the Bengal Ordinance; when he rejected overtures for a Round Table Conference; when he suggested another Royal Commission on the Constitution, tantamount to postponement of India's claims; and when the Labour party in opposition tamely supported the Tory Bill for bleeding India by increasing the emoluments to the British bureaucracy; and, finally, when the Parliamentary Committee of the Labour party adopted Mrs. Besant's Commonwealth of India Bill, an undemocratic measure both as to franchise and second chambers, and which the Indian National Congress refused to discuss, Indians were driven, against their will, to the conclusion that the Parliamentary Labour party was bitten with Imperialism, and that India could not rely upon it for the realisation of its goal of self-government.

The writer tried to reassure Indians, both on the public platform and in the Indian press, that the rank and file of the Labour movement in Great Britain was true to the great principle of Home Rule; that the resolutions passed at the annual meeting in 1925 of the Independent Labour party, of the Labour party, and of the Trades Union Congress, in favour of Home Rule for India, proved conclusively that their heart was in the right place; and that the next Labour Government would redeem Britain's pledges and give India her heart's desire.

Unless the Labour party realises that Imperialism is Capitalism writ large in force and fraud, unless Labour frees itself and England from this insidious and virulent poison, all its fondest hopes of Socialism in our time, of Nationalisation in our time, of elimination of the basest and most selfish and immoral attributes of private profiteering, are born in vain, and await the inevitable grave of imperialism.

Socialism in England seems difficult, if not impossible, while we hold India, because of the exportation of British capital to India, as illustrated by the migration of the mills of Dundee to Calcutta.

Imperialism being the greatest enemy of the British people as well as of the human race, the Labour party must slay this dragon before it can rescue the people of England and of the world.

It may appear a hard saying, but until India, Egypt, Ceylon, Irak, Kenya, and the other slave parts of the British Empire, enjoy self-government on the Australian and Canadian model, the British working classes do not deserve better conditions of life, do not deserve emancipation from economic slavery, for with political power in their hands, with the power to bend the British Parliament to their own will, their first duty is to undo the crimes committed by their country, and confer political freedom on the innumerable company of slaves in the British Empire. Until the leaders of Labour grasp this moral and put it into action they are little better than Prometheus chained to a rock, or popinjays in the hidden hand of imperial Capitalism.

Every member of the Labour party should repeat every morning Lamartine's famous words: "No man ever riveted a chain of slavery round his brother's neck but God silently welded the other end round the neck of the tyrant."

Every bishop and every minister of religion who prays for "peace on earth and goodwill to men" might appropriately repeat Lamartine's lines to his congregation until England breaks the fetters she has forged for India, Egypt, and other parts of God's world.

Towards a solution of the Indian problem, which all good men wish to bring about in the interests of England, of India, and of the world—world progress on a grand scale seems impossible as long as West dominates East by force and interferes with her self-expression and natural evolution—I submit the following principles:—

I. *In accord with the sacred principle of self-determination, India must draw up her own Constitution.*

The imperial dictation of England in 1919 disregarded India's right to shape her own Constitution, exhibited the cowardice and insincerity of British statesmanship, and transgressed against the vital principle of self-determination for which the Great War was fought

In the revision of the constitution there should be no repetition of that overbearing interference. India should revise or reframe her Constitution, and British Imperialists would be wise to put their insufferable pride in their pockets, remembering also that a nation which embodies a hereditary chamber in its Constitution is scarcely competent to advise, much less to dictate, a Constitution.

If the British Labour party sought to protect the masses of India by pressing for manhood or adult suffrage and no second chambers, I believe it would push at an open door, for the intelligentsia of India has learnt from the mistakes of Western Constitution-builders. Second chambers only make complete democratic government impossible, and bring parliamentary government into contempt.

With regard to the objection of the "illiteracy" of the masses, illiteracy is no legal barrier to exercising the vote in England and in other Western countries, and illiterates in India to-day vote under the present Constitution. Illiterates in India know how to vote, and, next to schools, the vote is the best means to break down illiteracy and to educate the people in self-government.

II. *There is no half-way house to self-government.* The framers of the 1919 Constitution ignominiously failed because they attempted the stupid trick of dual control (dyarchy). Divided control between Englishmen and Indians cannot work. Indians must be masters in their own house.

It may be necessary to make India a party question in British politics as Ireland was under Gladstone, and South Africa under Campbell-Bannerman, unless peradventure the Tory bear with a ring through its nose allows the Labour lamb to lead it. The Labour party has espoused the cause of Home Rule for India and, if any of its leaders, by conviction or cowardice, are opposed to this policy, duty demands that they should stand to one side and let others with greater faith in the healing, emancipating and uplifting powers of self-government lead the party and the nation on the high-road to freedom.

III. *Morally it does not lie in the province of England as conqueror and exploiter to determine the day and the season of India's emancipation from foreign rule, nor to determine whether India is fit for self-government or not. These vital rights belong to India, and her judgment should be accepted as final by England, if England has any respect for justice and liberty.* After more than four years of sanguinary conflict Germany was conquered, but her sovereign rights, with certain limited infractions, have been respected by the Allies, and now, within eight years of the Armistice, she has been restored as an equal amongst equals in the council of the nations.

After nearly a hundred and fifty years of devitalising and degenerating conquest andexploitation and overrule *India must be put in her rightful place, an equal amongst equals, and her sovereign rights acknowledged and accepted,* otherwise England stands condemned as a nation of hypocrites, and the greatest offender against freedom on the face of the earth.

If only England would approach India in the spirit of Locarno, the Indian problem would be solved without any more bitterness and bloodshed.

India and World Progress

The conclusion of the whole matter is that British domination over India forms the greatest barrier to freedom and progress in the world (1) by emasculating and suppressing the self-expression of one-fifth of the human race, and (2) by making the freedom of Egypt and of the Euphrates valley, not to mention that of

Malta, Cyprus, Ceylon, etc., wait upon the freedom of India. Indian freedom is the keystone to African and Asiatic freedom.

The British Empire is an audacious combination of freedom and slavery, and unless British statesmen free the slave nations under their control, one fears another great war to smash British Imperialism and to make the world safe for democracy.

> " O wad some power the giftie gie us
> To see oursels as others see us !
> It wad frae monie a blunder free us,
> And foolish notion."

It is recorded in the New Testament, which Englishmen profess to accept as the guide to individual and national conduct, that the devil took Christ up into a high mountain and showed Him the glittering prizes of dominion and empire, which the evil one promised should be his, if only Christ would fall down and worship him, when Christ rebuked the tempter and said, " Get thee behind Me, Satan."

Far otherwise was it with Great Britain when she was submitted by the devil to the same temptation and fell, and lost her own soul, unmindful of the crown that virtue gives, unmindful of her evil example, which has led other nations into the bloody scramble for empire and profits, unmindful of the greatest prizes in life: self-control, self-sacrifice and human service towards the supreme goal of peace and goodwill, of liberty, equality and fraternity.

I love my country ; I love India ; and my love for both constrains me to appeal to my countrymen to do unto Indians as they would that Indians should do unto them if conditions were reversed, if Indians were the conquerors and Englishmen the conquered.

INDEX